SpringerBriefs in Public Health

SpringerBriefs in Public Health present concise summaries of cutting-edge research and practical applications from across the entire field of public health, with contributions from medicine, bioethics, health economics, public policy, biostatistics, and sociology.

The focus of the series is to highlight current topics in public health of interest to a global audience, including health care policy; social determinants of health; health issues in developing countries; new research methods; chronic and infectious disease epidemics; and innovative health interventions.

Featuring compact volumes of 55 to 125 pages, the series covers a range of content from professional to academic. Possible volumes in the series may consist of timely reports of state-of-the art analytical techniques, reports from the field, snapshots of hot and/or emerging topics, literature reviews, and in-depth case studies. Both solicited and unsolicited manuscripts are considered for publication in this series.

Briefs are published as part of Springer's eBook collection, with millions of users worldwide. In addition, Briefs are available for individual print and electronic purchase.

Briefs are characterized by fast, global electronic dissemination, standard publishing contracts, easy-to-use manuscript preparation and formatting guidelines, and expedited production schedules. We aim for publication 8–12 weeks after acceptance.

Peter P. Groenewegen • Ilmo Keskimäki •
Alastair H. Leyland

Health Systems, Health Services and Inequality in Population Health

Peter P. Groenewegen
Netherlands Institute for Health Services
Research (Nivel)
Utrecht, The Netherlands

Alastair H. Leyland
MRC/CSO Social and Public Health
Sciences Unit, University of Glasgow
Glasgow, UK

Ilmo Keskimäki
Finnish Institute for Health and
Welfare (THL)
Helsinki, Finland

Faculty of Social Sciences
Tampere University
Tampere, Finland

ISSN 2192-3698 ISSN 2192-3701 (electronic)
SpringerBriefs in Public Health
ISBN 978-3-032-02564-7 ISBN 978-3-032-02565-4 (eBook)
https://doi.org/10.1007/978-3-032-02565-4

© The Editor(s) (if applicable) and The Author(s) 2026. This book is an open access publication.

Open Access This book is licensed under the terms of the Creative Commons Attribution 4.0 International License (http://creativecommons.org/licenses/by/4.0/), which permits use, sharing, adaptation, distribution and reproduction in any medium or format, as long as you give appropriate credit to the original author(s) and the source, provide a link to the Creative Commons license and indicate if changes were made.

The images or other third party material in this book are included in the book's Creative Commons license, unless indicated otherwise in a credit line to the material. If material is not included in the book's Creative Commons license and your intended use is not permitted by statutory regulation or exceeds the permitted use, you will need to obtain permission directly from the copyright holder.

The use of general descriptive names, registered names, trademarks, service marks, etc. in this publication does not imply, even in the absence of a specific statement, that such names are exempt from the relevant protective laws and regulations and therefore free for general use.

The publisher, the authors and the editors are safe to assume that the advice and information in this book are believed to be true and accurate at the date of publication. Neither the publisher nor the authors or the editors give a warranty, expressed or implied, with respect to the material contained herein or for any errors or omissions that may have been made. The publisher remains neutral with regard to jurisdictional claims in published maps and institutional affiliations.

This Springer imprint is published by the registered company Springer Nature Switzerland AG
The registered company address is: Gewerbestrasse 11, 6330 Cham, Switzerland

If disposing of this product, please recycle the paper.

Preface

The origin of this book lies in monthly online meetings that we started during the COVID-19 pandemic. We have known each other for a long time and discussed personal matters, politics, history, and everything else that came up. Of course, we also talked about our research and our research interests. During these discussions, the link between each of our main research interests came up. Peter is interested in health systems, Ilmo in health services, and Alastair in population health. Apart from that, we have a common interest in inequalities in health.

It struck us that even when visiting the same conference—the European Public Health Conference—we seldom found ourselves in the same sessions. Each of us lived and worked in our own silo. Our research areas have developed into separate disciplines. As researchers, we tend to specialise in our own disciplines with interaction between the three hampered by specialist journals and conferences (or even conference tracks) serving each separately.

In this book, we have brought together our research areas and our common interest in health inequalities. We hope that it will inspire others to look over the boundaries of their own specialisation and research area, to discuss and discover the added value of combining more or less separate research areas, and to engage in multidisciplinary research.

The primary audience for our book consists of researchers in health systems research, health services research, and population health research, but we also believe that our book is relevant for health policy researchers, health impact researchers, health economists and epidemiologists. However, we hope that it will also find an audience outside academia with practitioners and policymakers to improve understanding of how these different worlds collide.

The book is not intended as a textbook but can be used as additional reading for courses in many disciplines within social and health sciences, such as health and social policy, health systems and services research, and public health.

Enjoy reading!

Utrecht, Netherlands Peter P. Groenewegen
Helsinki, Finland Ilmo Keskimäki
Glasgow, Scotland Alastair H. Leyland

Acknowledgements

We thank Mariam Jack (University of Glasgow) for her help with some of the figures.

The ideas contained in this book were presented at two conferences, the European Public Health Conference in Berlin, November 2022, and the World Conference on Public Health in Rome, May 2023, and at a seminar at the Finnish Institute for Health and Welfare (THL) in Helsinki. We thank all participants at these occasions for their input. In particular, we would like to thank the discussants at the European Public Health Conference in Berlin in November 2022, Aileen Clarke, Alison McCallum, and Karsten Vrangbæk; and the discussants at the Helsinki seminar: Sakari Karvonen, Tuukka Tammi, Liina-Kaisa Tynkkynen, and Erkki Vartiainen.

A nearly final draft of the manuscript has been reviewed by Rachel Thomson and Vital Katikireddi (University of Glasgow), Laura Kihlström (THL), and Judith de Jong and Marloes Meijer (Nivel). We are very grateful for their comments.

We thank our institutions for paying to make this book open access.

AL was funded by the Medical Research Council (MC_UU_00022/2) and the Scottish Government Chief Scientist Office (SPHSU17).

Competing Interests The authors have no competing interests to declare that are relevant to the content of this manuscript.

Contents

1	**Health Systems Research, Health Services Research, and Population Health Research**...............................	1
	1.1 Introduction	1
	1.2 Health Systems Research..................................	4
	1.3 Health Services Research..................................	5
	1.4 Population Health Research...............................	6
	1.5 Overlapping Areas	7
	1.6 Our Aims and Approach...................................	8
	1.7 Conclusions	9
	References...	10
2	**Pathways Between Health Systems, Health Services, and Inequalities in Population Health**	13
	2.1 Introduction	13
	2.2 Pathways and Levels of Analysis........................	13
	2.3 Social Determinants of Health...........................	17
	2.4 Feedback Loops and Dynamics..........................	18
	2.5 Difficulty Separating Cause and Effect	19
	2.6 Link with the Chapters to Follow	20
	2.7 Conclusions	20
	References...	21
3	**Societal Values, Structures, and Institutions, and Their Impact on Health System Design**	23
	3.1 Introduction	23
	3.2 Types of Health Systems	25
	3.3 Health Systems and Broader Welfare Systems	28
	3.4 Core Characteristics of Health Systems................	29
	3.5 Priorities in Health Systems..............................	34
	3.6 Conclusions	35
	References...	35

4	**Health System Design and Inequalities in Population Health**	39
	4.1 Introduction	39
	4.2 The Contribution of Health Care to Population Health and Inequalities	41
	4.3 Health Expenditures and Inequalities in Population Health	42
	4.4 Complexity and Fragmentation of Health Systems	43
	4.5 Market Elements in Health Systems	44
	4.6 Primary Care and Equality	45
	4.7 Conclusions	47
	References	47
5	**Health System Design and Service Provision**	51
	5.1 Introduction	51
	5.2 Approachability	52
	5.3 Acceptability	54
	5.4 Availability and Accommodation	55
	5.5 Affordability	57
	5.6 Appropriateness	59
	5.7 Conclusions	60
	References	61
6	**Health Service Provision and Differential Service Utilization, Treatment, and Benefits**	63
	6.1 Introduction	63
	6.2 Gaining Access to Health Services	65
	Abilities to Perceive Need and to Seek Care	67
	Abilities to Reach and to Pay for Care	68
	Ability to Engage in Health Care	68
	6.3 Differences in Treatment and Care	69
	6.4 Differential Benefits from the Use of Health Services and their Life Course Accrual	73
	6.5 Conclusions	76
	References	77
7	**From Access to and Utilisation of Health Services to Equality in Population Health**	79
	7.1 Introduction	79
	7.2 Why Simple Aggregation May Not Work, and Potential Solutions	80
	7.3 What Is the Population?	81
	7.4 Quasi-Experiments and Natural Experiments	82
	7.5 Feedback Loops and Longitudinal Analysis	83
	7.6 Microsimulation and Agent-Based Models	84
	7.7 Health Impact Analysis	85
	7.8 Public Health Foresight Studies	85
	7.9 Conclusions	86
	References	86

8	**The Added Value of Integrating the Three Areas and the Way Forward**...		89
	8.1	The Substantive Question and the Intermediate Steps...........	89
	8.2	The Added Value of Combining Health Systems, Health Services, and Population Health Research................	91
	8.3	Elements of a Research Agenda............................	94
		Whole-System Approach................................	94
		Research Designs and Methodology	95
		Transformation of Inequalities in Population Health...........	95
		Specific Health Care Sectors	96
	8.4	Conditions for Integration and Collaboration	97
		First Solution: The Practical Organisation of Research.........	97
		Second Solution: Publication Venues and Conferences.........	98
		Third Solution: Capacity Building and Career Opportunities....	99
		Fourth Solution: Funding for Research That Integrates the Three Approaches...................................	99
	8.5	Conclusions	100
	References...		101
Index..			103

About the Authors

Peter P. Groenewegen is a sociologist. He is senior researcher 'Health systems and governance' and former director of the Netherlands Institute for Health Services Research (Nivel). He was an endowed professor at Utrecht University in the departments of sociology and human geography. His main research interests include international comparative studies of health systems, health policy, and health care organisation. (His publications can be found at https://www.nivel.nl/en/peter-groenewegen.)

Ilmo Keskimäki works as Research Professor at the Finnish Institute for Health and Welfare (THL) and is affiliated to the Tampere University as Professor of Health Services Research. His research has particularly focused on developing research methods for the use of register-based longitudinal data in health services research and for evaluating health system performance, and equity and effectiveness of health services. He is a Past President of the European Public Health Association (EUPHA) and currently serves as a medical editor of the *Finnish Medical Journal*. (His publications can be found at https://www.researchgate.net/profile/Ilmo-Keskimaeki/research.)

Alastair H. Leyland is Professor of Population Health Statistics and Associate Director of the MRC/CSO Social and Public Health Sciences Unit at the University of Glasgow, Scotland. He has led a programme on Inequalities in Health since 1999 and is co-Director of the NIHR Global Health Research Unit on Social and Environmental Determinants of Health Inequalities. He was an editor of the *European Journal of Public Health* from 2009 to 2023 and was one of the editors of the 7th edition of the *Oxford Textbook of Global Public Health*. (His publications can be found at https://eprints.gla.ac.uk/view/author/2063.html.)

List of Abbreviations

AI	Artificial Intelligence
AMI	Acute Myocardial Infarction
CMO	Context, Mechanisms, and Outcomes
CDoH	Commercial Determinants of Health
EU	European Union
GPs	General Practitioners
HSPA	Health System Performance Analysis
IKNL	Integraal Kankercentrum Nederland; Netherlands Comprehensive Cancer Organisation
IOM	Institute of Medicine
KNMG	Koninklijke Nederlanse Maatschappij ter bevordering van de Geneeskunst; Royal Dutch Medical Association
MAIHDA	Multilevel Analysis of Individual Heterogeneity and Discriminatory Accuracy
NACCHO	National Aboriginal Community Controlled Health Organisation
NH systems	National Health systems
NHS	UK National Health System
NICE	National Institute for Health and Care Excellence
OECD	Organisation for Economic Co-operation and Development
PRR	Populist Radical Right-wing
PVV	Party for Freedom – Partij Voor de Vrijheid
SES	Socio-Economic Status
SHI	Social Health Insurance
SDG	Sustainable Development Goals
UHC	Universal Health Coverage
UK	United Kingdom
US(A)	United States (of America)
WHO	World Health Organization

Chapter 1
Health Systems Research, Health Services Research, and Population Health Research

1.1 Introduction

Inequalities in health within countries are universal, but the magnitude of these inequalities varies between countries. In this book, we raise the question what role the design of health systems and the provision of health services play in creating and maintaining equality in population health. We do this against the background of our observation that these influences on population health inequalities are often neglected and that this may be a consequence of the separate development of health systems research, health services research, and population health research.

The terms 'health inequality' and 'health inequity' are used in different ways (see Box 1.1); in this book, we use the definition that

> Health inequalities are the systematic, avoidable and unfair differences in health outcomes that can be observed between populations, between social groups within the same population or as a gradient across a population ranked by social position [1]

Numerous methods are available to measure health inequalities [2, 3]. Comparisons of the performance of some of the different measures have reached different conclusions as to the utility of the measures [4, 5]. These may serve as a reminder of the complexity of the issue, where even basic concepts such as whether the appropriate measure is based on the assessment of absolute or relative measures can be a subjective judgement [6], and where the need to present results in an understandable and easily interpretable fashion may restrict the choices available.

> **Box 1.1 Health Inequality and Health Inequity**
> The terms 'health inequalities' and 'health disparities' are often considered synonymous and are used to describe differences in health between population groups. They may be used to indicate that differences in health exist—usually in ways that disfavour groups that are disadvantaged socially, economically, or in other ways—but without necessarily implying causality. However, the very existence of such differences is likely to lead to an exploration of whether there is a causal relationship with health or with the determinants of health [7]. Health inequity is then sometimes used to distinguish the subset of health inequalities that can be considered unjust or unfair [8]; in this sense, inequalities are distinguished from inequities in that the former term does not imply a moral judgement [9]. Different definitions of health equity have been proposed for different audiences, depending in part on the underlying goal (e.g. describing health equity to a particular audience or as principles for monitoring progress towards health equity) [7]. However, the terms inequality and inequity are also often used interchangeably by some authors [10]. A recent review of the literature reported that the use of the two terms varied geographically, with 'health inequity' being more common in the Americas and 'health inequalities' prevailing in Europe [1]. In this book, we use the term 'health inequalities' with the definition provided in McCartney et al.'s review: 'Health inequalities are the systematic, avoidable and unfair differences in health outcomes that can be observed between populations, between social groups within the same population or as a gradient across a population ranked by social position' [1].

As a focus of health policy in many governments, health inequalities are widely studied in public health research. Explanations for health inequalities are sought in health behaviours, such as smoking or lack of physical activity, as more direct or 'downstream' influences. Behind these downstream explanations for health inequalities are the upstream explanations in terms of access to resources, such as education, housing, or work, that in turn are determined by societal structures, including institutional discrimination against certain categories of people. The upstream influences on health inequalities are called structural determinants of health, while the downstream explanations in terms of health behaviours and their direct determinants are called the social determinants of health. The World Health Organisation defines the social determinants of health broader as: 'the circumstances in which people are born, grow up, live, work and age, and the systems put in place to deal with illness. These circumstances are in turn shaped by a wider set of forces: economics, social policies, and politics' (https://www.who.int/news-room/questions-and-answers/item/social-determinants-of-health-key-concepts). This definition includes the health system and health services. However, studies of health inequalities too often ignore the role that health systems and health services play in

1.1 Introduction

inequalities in population health and, as a consequence, their potential to create or reduce inequalities in health. In our view, the reason for this is that research in these areas—population health research, health services research, and health systems research—have become siloed as academic disciplines. Researchers tend to specialise in their own field of research, with interaction between the three research areas hampered by specialist journals and conferences serving each separately. There is perhaps a mutual relationship between silos in research and the separation between health systems, health service provision, and population health in policy and in practice. Health policy is siloed with, e.g., separate departments in ministries of health. Practice is siloed with a lack of relationships between local or regional public health authorities and health service providers, and siloed specialisms in hospitals, posing problems for patients who have multiple care and care-related social needs. The matter is further complicated by the perception of the public, and frequently of policy makers, that equates health with health services meaning that treatment is prioritised over prevention.

This book has two aims. The first aim is to give an overview of what is known in the scientific literature about the relationships between the design and structure of health systems, health service provision and utilisation, and inequalities in population health. In doing so, our focus is mainly on high-income countries. This is not because low- and middle-income countries are not important, nor is it because health inequalities do not exist within low- and middle-income countries (they do), but because of the simple fact that our own research was done in, and mainly focused on, high-income countries. As such we are better acquainted with the literature on these countries. The second aim is to show the scientific and policy added value of combining health systems, health services, and population health research and to explore ways to overcome the silos they are now in. In doing so, we hope to create awareness among researchers to look beyond the boundaries of their own research field and promote multidisciplinary collaboration. We will deal with this second aim only in the final chapter (Chap. 8) of this book. We first have to give an overview of the relationships between health systems, health service provision, and inequalities in population health in order to be able to address the second aim in an informed way.

Based on the research literature and our own experience, we will give an overview of the relationships between health system design and inequalities in health and how this relationship can be understood. We, as authors, have experience in population health research (AL), health systems research (PG), and health services research (IK).

We hope to show the scientific and policy added value of combining health systems, health services, and population health research. After reading this book, researchers will be more aware of the approaches in the three areas and more inclined to look beyond the boundaries of their own field of research. In the final chapter, we will also discuss ways of breaking down the barriers between the three research fields.

1.2 Health Systems Research

Health systems research and the comparative analysis of health policies is defined as the research area 'that seeks to understand and improve how societies organise themselves in achieving collective health goals, and how different actors interact in the policy and implementation processes to contribute to policy outcomes'. [11] This definition distinguishes two broad areas of health systems research. The first area addresses questions about how health systems are organised and how they develop, while the second area focuses on the effects of health systems, such as improvement of health of the population. Health systems research includes financing and payment models that directly affect the possibilities of people to use health care services. In this book, we use the term health system *design* for how health systems are structured and funded. This underpins that the structure and funding of health systems is not some given situation but has come about at least partly through political decisions and actions of parties in the health system.

Often a distinction is made between health systems and health *care* systems, where the first relates to the whole of systems and policies that contribute to health (e.g. including housing policies and road safety measures) or have the intention to improve or maintain health through 'health actions' [12]. Health care systems refer, more narrowly, to the system of health service provision. The latter does include prevention and health promotion as far as they are provided as a health service to individuals or groups of individuals (in group health care sessions). Hence, we exclude general media campaigns on the benefits of physical activity but include vaccination campaigns. The focus of this book is on health care systems, hence the narrower definition; however, the health system will be discussed when we address the wider social determinants of health that—in addition to health care—influence population health. The wider social determinants of health are central to the idea of health in all policies [13]. In this approach, policies in all areas of government should be evaluated in terms of their consequences for people's health, for example, by health impact assessment [14]. We will come back to health impact assessment in Chap. 7 where we discuss the step from individual outcomes to population health inequalities: 'From access and utilisation of health services to inequalities in population health'.

It should be noted that the concept of health care system has a different meaning in Europe and the United States. In Europe, health care systems coincide with countries. Usually there is one main health care system in each country, although this should not be taken for granted with federal states, such as Germany, or autonomous regions, such as in Spain. Regional health systems may differ in important respects [15]. In the US, health care systems refer to hospitals and physicians that are affiliated with one organisation [16]. They are defined as 'a group of health care organisations (e.g. physician practices, hospitals, skilled nursing facilities) that are jointly owned or managed' [17]. These organisations have different sizes, from small local organisations to large organisations that cross the boundaries of states. Although there is increasing research on the performance of these health care systems and their advantages and disadvantages compared to health care provision that is not part of a health care system, there is much less information about their structural features and how these may be explained [17]. Federal policies and regulations in the US contribute to health system characteristics as they are usually understood in the European context [18].

Despite these terminological distinctions, usually the term health system is used both in the research literature and in policy discussions. We will therefore also use the shorter term health system in this book, unless there is a risk of confusion.

1.3 Health Services Research

Health services research, in a well-known definition, 'is the multidisciplinary field of scientific investigation that studies how social factors, financing systems, organisational structures and processes, health technologies, and personal behaviours affect access to health care, the quality and cost of health care, and ultimately our health and well-being' [19]. While health systems research focuses on the health system itself, health services research is concerned with the utilisation of services, the factors influencing this utilisation, and its impact on individuals, populations, and their health outcomes.

The key objectives of health services research include: [20]

- Understanding health care delivery: examining how different health care settings, systems, and practices affect patient outcomes and the overall performance of the health care system.
- Evaluating interventions: assessing the effectiveness, safety, and cost-effectiveness of medical treatments, technologies, and health care delivery models.
- Investigating factors influencing access to health care services, particularly for underserved populations, and identifying ways to reduce disparities in care.
- Analysing the impact of health policies and regulations on health care delivery and population health.
- Examining resource allocation within health care systems and identifying strategies to improve the efficiency and effectiveness of care.

Compared to health systems research, which typically focuses on macro-level issues within health systems, health services research addresses more meso- and micro-level questions. These might include specific interventions, new services, the relationship between patients and providers, or even the operations of a particular hospital or network of providers. Additionally, while health systems research generally aims to enhance the overall performance of the system, health services research usually focuses on supporting the delivery of care and improving patient outcomes for specific interventions and services.

The design of the health system—whether services are publicly or privately provided and financed—along with major social, political, and public health challenges, can shape the content of health services research conducted in a given country. In some countries, health services research emphasises clinical issues, the adoption of new interventions, and health technology. In others, the research questions may align more closely with health systems research, addressing issues related to system reforms, prioritisation, and resource allocation.

Population health and its distribution within society are usually not the primary focus of health services research. However, this field does investigate the mechanisms and processes that link the characteristics of health systems and health care to population health and its disparities.

1.4 Population Health Research

Inequalities in health are part of population health. Kindig and Stoddart [21] defined population health as 'the health outcomes of a group of individuals, including the distribution of such outcomes within the group', with this covering health outcomes, the patterning of the determinants of health, and the manner in which policies and interventions link these. In Whitehead and Dahlgren's [22] definition '[s]ocial inequities in health are systematic differences in health status between different socio-economic groups'. Within population health research, health equity research is defined as 'research which improves the understanding of issues that influence the distribution of health and healthcare within populations. This includes the discussion of political, policy-related, economic, social and health systems- and services-related influences, particularly with regard to identifying and understanding the systematic differences or the lived experiences of one or more aspects of health in population groups defined demographically, geographically, or socially' [23]. This definition puts health and healthcare inequalities under one umbrella. However, the logic behind these concepts differs. Equity in health has a normative background as a value in itself (see Box 1.1). Social inequalities in health '… are systematic, socially produced (and therefore modifiable) and unfair' [22]. This links social inequalities in health to societal values that also influence the health system of a country. However, what is considered fair in terms of health services may vary more across societies than the views on inequalities in health. Differences in health care utilisation may reflect differences in need, demand, and preferences of people and are not always or necessarily seen as unfair.

The study of health inequalities requires the study of different population groups, however defined. This is in contrast to the practice of clinical medicine, which focuses on the treatment of individual patients. The population groups studied are assumed to some extent to be homogenous in their characteristics. Individuals within a group will, however, differ in their outcomes; individuals will or will not have a given disease at a point in time but, collectively, the group will have a specific prevalence of disease.

Often the population groups in health inequalities research are defined in terms of income, education, or ethnic background. However, there are more group

1.5 Overlapping Areas

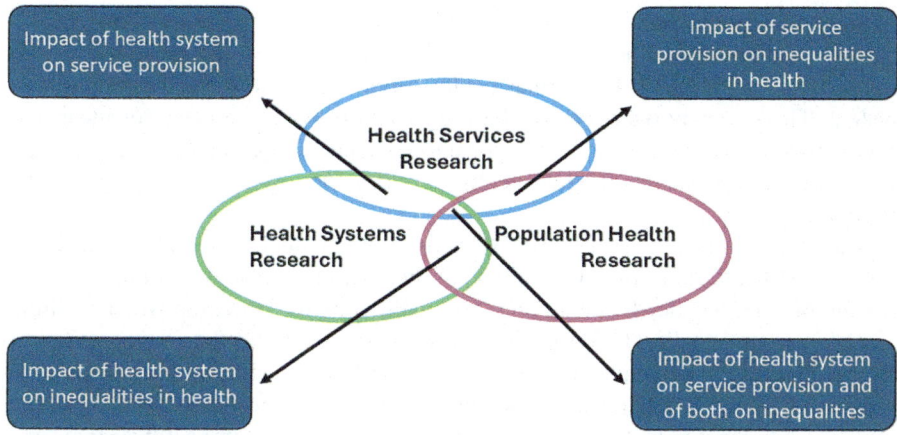

Fig. 1.1 Overlapping areas between health systems research, health services research, and population health research

characteristics that relate to inequalities in health and there may be specific combinations, also called intersections, of different population groups that are important in the study of health inequalities [24]. Intersectionality is a theoretical framework that enables us to understand how different social identities (such as race or ethnicity, gender, socioeconomic position, and sexual orientation) combine at the individual level in ways that lead to different experiences of societal privilege and oppression [25]. This goes beyond treating the impact of social identities as additive to acknowledge that the effect of these overlapping identities may create unique additional interactions. In recent years, intersectionality has moved beyond the theoretical to be used as an analytical tool to address structural inequalities [26]. Intersectionality can be analysed using Multilevel Analysis of Individual Heterogeneity and Discriminatory Accuracy (MAIHDA), which provides several advantages over the more conventional use of interactions in regression models [27].

Since health systems are societal constructs, the systems and structures of oppression that are contained within a society can be reflected in its health system and can create, perpetuate, or exaggerate inequalities in population health [28].

1.5 Overlapping Areas

In Fig. 1.1, we have depicted the three research areas of population health, health systems, and health services research in a Venn diagram to show the overlapping areas that we focus on. The overlaps are important because they indicate areas that cannot be resolved using just insights from one of these three research areas. Moreover, they indicate domains through which it is possible to tackle health inequalities.

There may not be much overlap between all three areas of health systems, health services, and population health inequality research. For a start, inequalities in health are determined by much more than health service provision and the health care system. The two-way overlaps will be bigger and provide the basis for ideas and hypotheses on how, e.g., health systems influence health inequalities at population level through access to effective health services for low-income groups in the population.

The impact of health service utilisation on health inequalities will be small when we think of health in terms of incidence of disease, given also the minimal role of prevention due to under-financing in most health systems. However, when we think in terms of case fatality, functional capacity, or more broadly the consequences of disease, the impact of health services is larger [29]. The extent to which health service provision and utilisation impact on health inequalities may differ between countries. On the whole, European countries have relatively fair health systems and their populations and politics tend to support equitable values and goals, which is reflected in their health (care) systems and in a supranational institution such as the European Union (EU) [30]. The impact of health care will be different in health systems that do not provide free or inexpensive access to health services and operate on the principle of willingness and ability to pay.

1.6 Our Aims and Approach

In this book, we explore these connections between health systems, health services, and inequalities in health care utilisation, and population health at a conceptual level, using our own research experience and the broader literature. We did not perform a large integrative empirical research project; the reasons for this will be clear from Chap. 7. We will review the existing literature—without claiming to be exhaustive—in order to identify mechanisms and pathways that may link health system design, organisation of service delivery, and population health inequalities. Chapter 2 will outline these pathways and the heuristic scheme we use there will guide the organisation of the book. As we said, our focus is on the literature about health systems of high-income countries. In doing so, our aim is to show the scientific and policy added value of combining health systems, health services, and population health research, to create awareness among researchers to look over the boundaries of their own research field, and to promote multidisciplinary collaboration.

We will consider diverse outcomes, because these may differ according to the focus on general or disease-specific mechanisms and pathways. Outcomes may be generic relating to (self-reported) ill health or functional capabilities, or they may be disease specific, such as the incidence of specific diseases and the functional consequences of these or relate to the (patient reported) outcomes of treatment.

There are several arguments why our particular focus is relevant. The three research areas that we cover have to some extent become silos, as a result of specialisation of researchers, the way that research is funded, the journals in which they publish, and the conferences that they attend. In respect of the last two points the European Journal of Public Health is an example of a journal in which researchers from all three areas publish. The European Public Health Conference is an example of a conference at which researchers from all three fields are present (although this is not reflected in the names of the journal or conference), but this does not guarantee that they work together on integrative topics.

In each of these areas, researchers with a different mix of disciplinary backgrounds are active. Health systems research is largely international comparative research and often, but certainly not exclusively, done by researchers with a background in the social sciences, economics, and political science. Health services research varies strongly in the disciplinary background of its researchers, and, in some countries, it is strongly clinically led. The research area of health inequalities in the population is largely the domain of social epidemiologists but draws on many disciplines. As a result of the different mix of disciplines, with different approaches and different cultures of doing research and publishing, health systems research, health services research, and population health research have tended to grow apart and to ignore the results from the other areas. This book is therefore a call for increased collaboration across the disciplines.

1.7 Conclusions

- Studies of health inequalities too often ignore the role that health systems and health services play in population health and their potential to create or reduce inequalities in health.
- Population health research, health services research, and health systems research have become siloed as academic specialisations.
- There are two broad areas of health systems research: how health systems are organised and how they develop, and the effects of health systems, such as improvement of health of the population.
- Health services research studies the organisation of health care provision and its effects on utilisation and health outcomes.
- Population health research studies the conditions under which populations can be healthy and how health is distributed in the population.
- These three areas of research overlap but the extent of overlap is unknown.
- Our aim is to show the added value of combining the three areas, to create awareness among researchers to look over the boundaries of their own field of research, and to promote multidisciplinary collaboration.

References

1. McCartney G, Popham F, McMaster R, Cumbers A. Defining health and health inequalities. Public Health. 2019;172:22–30.
2. Regidor E. Measures of health inequalities: part 1. J Epidemiol Community Health. 2004;58:858–61.
3. Regidor E. Measures of health inequalities: part 2. J Epidemiol Community Health. 2004;58:900–3.
4. Wagstaff A, Paci P, Van Doorslaer EKA. On the measurement of inequalities in health. Soc Sci Med. 1991;33:545–57.
5. Mackenbach J, Kunst AE. Measuring the magnitude of socio-economic inequalities in health: an overview of available measures illustrated with two examples from Europe. Soc Sci Med. 1997;44:757–71.
6. Asada Y. A framework for measuring health inequity. J Epidemiol Community Health. 2005;59:700–5.
7. Braveman P, Arkin E, Orleans T, Proctor D, Acker J, Plough A. What is health equity? Behav Sci Policy. 2018;4:1–14.
8. Braveman P, Gruskin S. Defining equity in health. J Epidemiol Community Health. 2003;57:254–8.
9. Kawachi I, Subramanian SV, Almeida-Filho N. A glossary for health inequalities. J Epidemiol Community Health. 2002;56:647–52.
10. Krieger NA. A glossary for social epidemiology. J Epidemiol Community Health. 2001;55:693–700.
11. Alliance for Health Policy and Systems Research. What is HPSR? Overview Geneva: World Health Organisation; 2011 [Available from: https://www.who.int/alliance-hpsr/about/hpsr/en/]
12. Murray CJL, Frenk J. A framework for assessing the performance of health systems. Bull World Health Organ. 2000;78(6):717–31.
13. Greer SL, Falkenbach M, Siciliani L, McKee M, Wismar M, Vissapragada P, et al. Making Health for All Policies. Harnessing the co-benefits of health. Copenhagen: European Observatory on Health Systems and Policies; 2023.
14. Wanjohi NW, Harrison R, Harris-Roxas B. Health impact assessments of health sector proposals: an audit and narrative synthesis. Int J Environ Res Public Health. 2021;18:11466.
15. Amelina A, Nergiz DD, Faist T, Glick Schiller N, editors. Beyond methodological nationalism: research methodologies for cross-border studies. Routledge; 2012.
16. Kronick R. The promise and peril of health systems. Health Serv Res. 2020;55:1027–30.
17. Beaulieu ND, Chernew ME, McWilliams JM, Landrum MB, Dalton M, Yutong GA, et al. Organization and performance of US Health Systems. JAMA. 2023;329(4):325–35.
18. Rice T, Rosenau P, Unruh LY, Barnes AJ, van Ginneken E. United States of America: Health system review. Health Syst Transit. 2020;22:i–441.
19. Lohr KN, Steinwachs DM. Health services research: an evolving definition of the field. Health Serv Res. 2002;37(1):15–7.
20. Wensing M, Ullrich C, editors. Foundations of health services research: principles, methods, and topics. Springer Nature; 2023.
21. Kindig D, Stoddart G. What is population health? American Journal of Public Health. 2003;93:380–3.
22. Whitehead M, Dahlgren G. Concepts and principles for tackling social inequities in health. Copenhagen: WHO Regional Office for Europe; 2006.
23. IJEH. Aims and scope: Int J Equity Health; 2021 [cited 2021 3 March]. Available from: https://equityhealthj.biomedcentral.com/about.
24. Krieger NA. Advancing gender transformative intersectional science for health justice: An ecosocial analysis. Soc Sci Med. 2024;351
25. Bowleg L. The problem with the phrase women and minorities: intersectionality-an important theoretical framework for public health. Am J Public Health. 2012;102:1267–73.

References

26. Bowleg L. Evolving intersectionality within public health: from analysis to action. Am J Public Health. 2021;111:88–90.
27. Evans CR, Leckie G, Subramanian SV, Bell A, Merlo J. A tutorial for conducting intersectional multilevel analysis of individual heterogeneity and discriminatory accuracy (MAIHDA). SSM Popul Health. 2024;26:101664.
28. Young R, Ayiasi RM, Shung-King M, Morgan R. Health systems of oppression: applying intersectionality in health systems to expose hidden inequities. Health Policy Plan. 2020;35:1228–30.
29. Starfield B. Pathways of influence on equity in health. Soc Sci Med. 2007;64:1355–62.
30. EU. Council conclusions on common values and principles in European Union Health Systems. Brussels: Council of the European Union; 2006.

Open Access This chapter is licensed under the terms of the Creative Commons Attribution 4.0 International License (http://creativecommons.org/licenses/by/4.0/), which permits use, sharing, adaptation, distribution and reproduction in any medium or format, as long as you give appropriate credit to the original author(s) and the source, provide a link to the Creative Commons license and indicate if changes were made.

The images or other third party material in this chapter are included in the chapter's Creative Commons license, unless indicated otherwise in a credit line to the material. If material is not included in the chapter's Creative Commons license and your intended use is not permitted by statutory regulation or exceeds the permitted use, you will need to obtain permission directly from the copyright holder.

Chapter 2
Pathways Between Health Systems, Health Services, and Inequalities in Population Health

2.1 Introduction

The substantive question we address in this book is whether and how health systems influence inequalities in population health. Health systems and inequalities in population health refer to the macro level of societies. This requires a comparative perspective on health systems. To understand how this influence comes about, we look at the pathways that run via other levels: health service provision at the meso level, and the actual service delivery and the utilisation of services which take place at the micro level where health care providers and users interact. The results of these interactions are, e.g., decisions on whether or not to use certain types of care and these decisions are patterned by socioeconomic characteristics of patients. These decisions form patterns of inequalities in population health at the macro level. We look at the health system as a social institution with certain design characteristics that may influence inequalities in population health and not as employer. Some health care systems—those with the health workforce as employees—can have a direct effect on inequalities. In 2021, an estimated 10.5% of jobs in OECD countries were in the health or social care sectors [1].

2.2 Pathways and Levels of Analysis

As stated above, the big question relates to the macro level of health care systems and inequalities in population health. There is a long tradition of studying the social determinants of health, e.g., the impact of the education system or the labour market on health outcomes, resulting in accumulated knowledge [2–4]. The stock of knowledge about whether or not and how the design of health systems and the organisation of health care influence inequalities in population health is much smaller [5]. To understand how this influence at macro level comes about, we need intermediate steps that run via service provision and utilisation at meso and micro level. Figure 2.1 illustrates this based on a heuristic model developed by Coleman [6, 7] (see Fig. 2.1). We will use this figure to structure Chaps. 3 through 7.

The macro-level relationship is indicated by the horizontal arrow between the health care system design on the left side and inequalities in population health on the right side of Fig. 2.1. The intermediate steps run through health service providers, located at the intermediate or meso level and their actual service delivery at the micro level where health care providers and users come together. Both health care providers and (potential) users of services bring their own attitudes, beliefs, abilities, and other resources that influence their interaction and together with the health system design influence their choice situations, e.g. in terms of the range of choices they have or perceive. The term micro level does not imply that we see users of health care as isolated individuals; to the contrary, their attitudes and beliefs are formed and reproduced within their families, wider social networks and the social and material resources they have (or lack). Users of health care may also differ in health as a result of social determinants of health (see Sect. 2.3).

Both meso and micro levels are influenced by macro-level structures and institutions, in society in general as well as in the design of the health system. The results of the interactions between health care providers and health care users (the micro level) are, e.g., decisions on whether or not to use certain types of care and these decisions may be patterned by socioeconomic characteristics of patients. These decisions usually cannot be aggregated directly. They require a more complicated

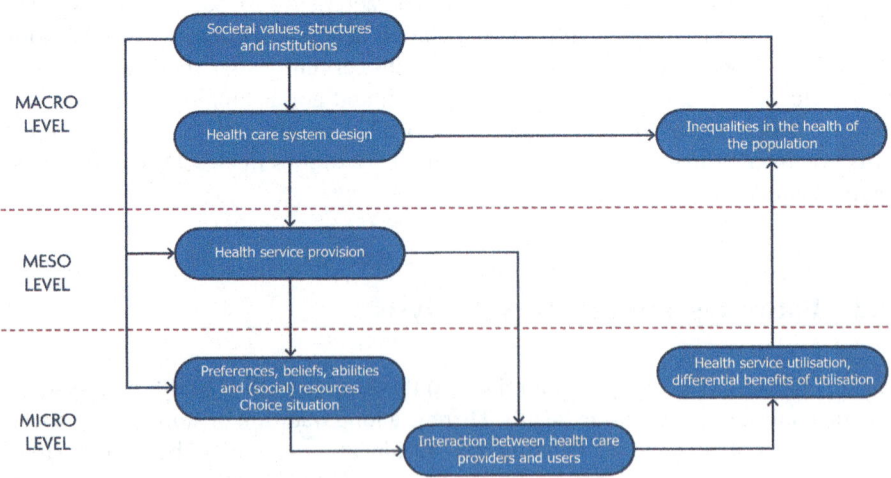

Fig. 2.1 Levels of analysis in the study of the impacts of health systems on service provision and the impact of both on inequalities in population health

2.2 Pathways and Levels of Analysis

transformation, e.g., a simulation model, into patterns of inequalities in population health at macro level, as we will discuss in Chap. 7.

The scheme in this figure acknowledges the much-studied influence of societal structures and institutions on inequalities in health at population level. Our focus in this book is on the role of health care systems and service provision as determinants of inequalities in population health, among many others. The fact that we have placed 'societal values, structures and institutions' in this scheme allows us to consider that societal values, structures, and institutions influence inequalities in population health via their influence on the health system and health service provision; in other words, the arrows from societal values, structures, and institutions to health system design and to health service provision represent what we could call the social determinants of health systems and service provision.

The relationship between the health care system design and inequalities in health in the population refers to what Papanicolas et al. [8] have called health system equity: the distribution of health improvement and people centredness across the population as a whole, as well as the level of financial protection. In the same way, the relationship between health service provision and service utilisation refers to health service equity: the distribution of the quality of the provided care and ensuring that it does not vary because of personal characteristics, such as gender, ethnicity, geographic location, and socioeconomic status [8].

At the micro level, we find the interactions between care providers and users. These interactions result in decisions about health service utilisation and treatments. Individual attitudes, beliefs, and abilities are not only shaped by broader societal processes, but also by health service provision and how this is organised. Health service provision shapes the expectations of (potential) health care users. Some people may refrain from health care utilisation because of the accessibility to the system (not only in physical or financial terms, but also psychologically and culturally), as witnessed during the COVID-19 pandemic, and the responsiveness of service providers. During the pandemic, some services were closed or accessible under special rules to prevent infection among patients (waiting rooms were often closed, because distance could not be held) or between patients and care providers. Patients delayed seeking care not only because of actual restrictions, but also because of fear of contagion. Patients' attitudes and beliefs may be socially patterned and hence contribute to inequalities in health care utilisation. Moreover, patients may benefit differentially from health care utilisation and treatment, depending on their capabilities.

Figure 2.1 describes—in an abstract way—the pathways between health system design and population health inequalities. A concrete example of a framework for understanding the unequal impact of COVID-19 on people from ethnic minorities, compared to people from the majority population, is described in Box 2.1.

Box 2.1 Pathways to Ethnic Inequalities in Health Outcomes During the COVID-19 Pandemic

The impact of COVID-19 differed between ethnic groups and the majority population in several countries. To identify pathways that have led to ethnic inequalities in COVID-19 health outcomes, Katikireddi and colleagues developed a framework (see Fig. 2.2) [9]. Structural racism and power structures are the macro-level context that explain why people from ethnic minorities are, e.g., differentially exposed to infection risk in their work or housing context (meso level), resulting in infection with the disease (individual-level outcome). The sum of the individual-level outcomes, aggregated over people from ethnic minorities and people from the majority population, shows the pattern and extent of inequalities.

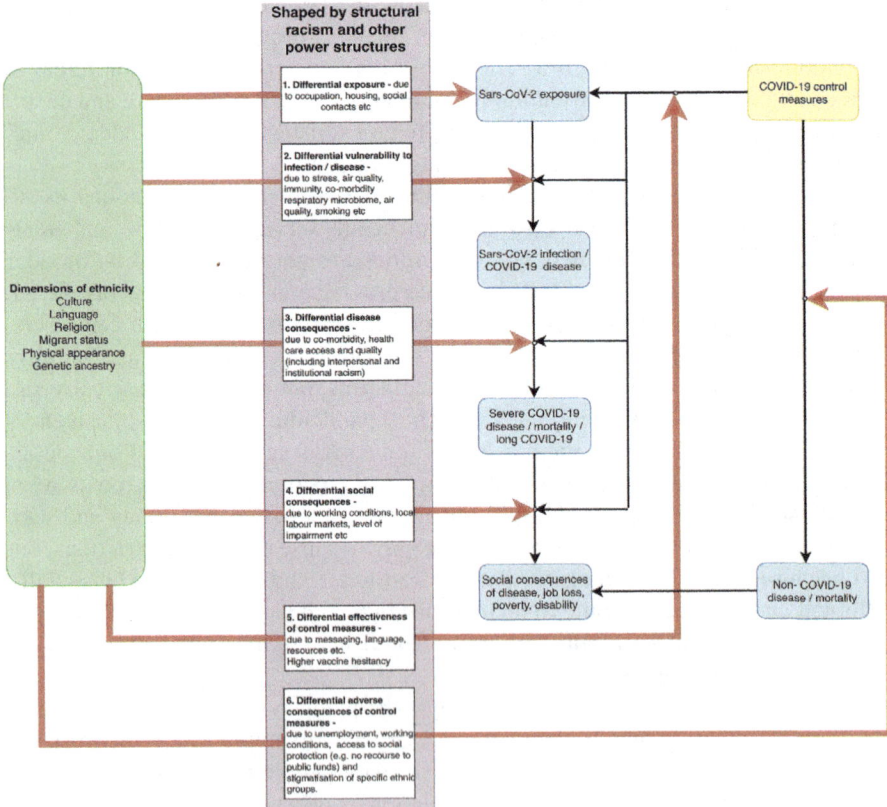

Fig. 2.2 Pathways underpinning ethnic inequalities in COVID-19. Source: Reproduced from Katikireddi et al. [9], Figure 1. https://doi.org/10.1136/jech-2020-216061, licensed under the terms of the Creative Commons Attribution 4.0 Unported (CC BY 4.0) license (https://creativecommons.org/licenses/by/4.0/)

Pathways are also often conceptualised in terms of the relationships between context, mechanisms, and outcomes (CMO) [10]. The approach sketched in Fig. 2.1 has advantages over the CMO-model. The explicit distinction between levels in Fig. 2.1 is important from an analytical point of view. Mechanisms may not exclusively be located at the micro level but also at meso and macro level and in the relationships between levels.

2.3 Social Determinants of Health

The focus of this book is on the influence of health systems and health service provision on inequalities in population health. However, the larger part of inequalities in population health are caused by the social determinants of health, as indicated in the upper part of Fig. 2.1 with the arrow from societal values, structures, and institutions to inequalities in health of the population. Therefore, we briefly discuss the social determinants of health in this section.

The social determinants of health are 'the conditions in which people are born, grow, work, live, and age, and the wider set of forces and systems shaping the conditions of daily life' [11]. These non-medical factors have a major influence on health and health inequalities. People's immediate environments, such as their homes and places of work, may have direct impact upon physical health; moreover, the impact of such environments may be heightened at critical stages of the life course such as pregnancy or childhood. But the inter-linked factors such as income, employment, and educational status will in part determine the distribution of resources (such as the ability to afford healthy foods or essential services) that will impact upon health [12]. Reducing inequalities in population health is therefore dependent on changing the ways in which societal values, structures, and institutions frame the social determinants of health and therefore impact on health behaviours and health itself. We can distinguish between the social factors that influence health and the social processes that lead to the unequal distribution of these health determinants across different social groups [13].

The health care system itself is a social determinant of health, being a societal construct that influences health and inequalities in health. How health care is accessed, experiences of interacting with it, and the benefits that are ultimately derived from it may vary according to gender, education, occupation, income, ethnicity, and place of residence [14]. It is not difficult to see how health system characteristics such as the means of financing the health system or the required level of out-of-pocket spending on health care have the potential to affect inequalities in health.

The Commission on Social Determinants of Health made three overarching recommendations for action to reduce inequalities in health: to improve the conditions of daily life; to tackle the inequitable distribution of power, money, and resources; and to measure and understand the problem and assess the impact of action [2].

2.4 Feedback Loops and Dynamics

Figure 2.1 presents a static picture of the relationships where inequalities are reproduced, but we also have to be aware of feedback loops from the outcomes at the right side of Fig. 2.1 to society, the health system, health service provision and utilisation. Health systems are complex systems (see also Chap. 7). Feedback loops can best be studied through changes over time, in other words a dynamic approach. Awareness among health care providers and patients of differential benefits of treatments for patients with a different socioeconomic background may change the behaviour of patients and of health care providers (see Fig. 2.3). This figure sketches three scenarios. In the first one, the system reproduces itself; the social and health system context influences the behaviours and interactions of patients and care providers; and the outcomes show more or less disparities in care and health. The second scenario sketches the situation in which care providers and/or patients are aware of the results of their behaviours and interactions and consequently adapt their behaviour. In other words, there is a feedback loop between the outcomes and the behaviours or interactions. For example, there is increasing awareness among health care providers of differences between patients in health literacy and they may act on this by following educational courses on communication with low health literacy patients [16]. Patients may act upon the benefits—or lack of them—of the treatment they receive by talking to their care provider about this or by choosing another care provider [17]. These feedback loops change the interactions between health service providers and patients and may affect outcomes in future points in time. The third scenario sketches a further feedback loop. The micro-level outcomes and the population health inequalities may also feed back to the system and societal level through awareness among policy makers and politicians. This may bring about changes in the health system through political decisions, for example, regarding the level of cost-sharing.

The reconstruction of explanatory pathways may be, on the one hand, rather general, for example, when we discuss the role of universal health coverage in increasing access to care and decreasing health inequalities, or, on the other hand,

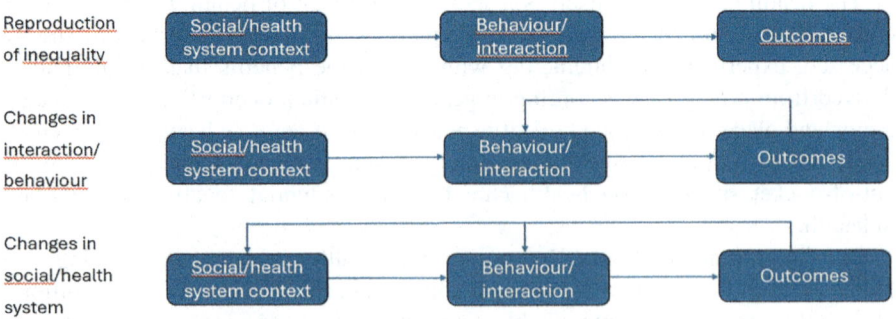

Fig. 2.3 Reproduction of inequalities, changes in behaviour and interaction at micro level, and changes in the social and health system. Source: authors' adaption based on [15]

developed along specific examples of diseases (or disease groups), such as coronary heart disease. In the case of general approaches, we would think of the social patterning of ill-health, combined with a lack of other resources and capabilities, that influences health-seeking behaviour and access to effective care. People with less education and on lower income have fewer resources to use health care effectively, may have poorer self-management capabilities, and are perhaps less likely to be referred to secondary care than would be suggested by their need for care. In addition, even in countries with overtly universal coverage, structural features in their health systems may favour the better-off in access to services. These features include factors such as the high impact of voluntary health insurance in several countries [18], parallel provision schemes as in Finland [19], or patient choice arrangements such as in Sweden [20].

Reconstructing explanatory pathways in the disease-specific case could start from the creation of populations at increased risk. For example, those surviving an acute myocardial infarction (AMI) are at increased risk of a subsequent AMI. People with low socioeconomic status (SES) are at increased risk of having an AMI. Among those who have an AMI, those of low SES are at increased risk of death, creating a social gradient in this population at increased risk. The first step, increased risk of AMI, may be largely determined by influences outside the health care system (but the inclusion of lifestyle altering programmes in health care—such as smoking cessation services—may 'endogenise' these influences into the health care system); however, for the second step (reoccurrence and survival) pathways will be more related to access to care and quality of service provision [21].

2.5 Difficulty Separating Cause and Effect

An advantage of Fig. 2.1 is that it facilitates the development of hypotheses and the multilevel methodology to test them. When we come to think about testable hypotheses, the diagram also shows the difficulty that we face—using a natural experiment or observational design within one country or health system, it may not be possible to separate the social determinants of health and of health systems, as the design of the health system is influenced by the same social structures. In other words, the same cultural and political determinants of inequalities in health also influence the design of health systems (including how they are funded) and the provision of health care services. This makes it difficult to test the impact of the health system in isolation from the broader societal structures. Nevertheless, there are also examples of divergent systems within the same society. We mention four here. A first example is the United Kingdom (UK), where different societal values shape the health care system and the welfare system; the National Health Service is seen as an expression of equal access to services while the cash transfers in the welfare system in the UK are seen as expression of liberal and conservative values [22]. A second example is Finland where municipal health care mirrors values of universal access, while at the same time the occupational health care system provides an alternative pathway to, e.g., primary care services based on employment and occupation [19, 23]. Third, in the past (and still in some cases now), there were parallel systems in the (former) Soviet countries with separate health care systems for workers in some crucial sectors, party apparatchiks, and the military [24]. Finally, dental care is an example of a health service sector that operates on different principles in many health systems, with little insurance coverage and much cost-sharing. The marginal position of dental care in health care systems and service provision seems to be related to the low value attached to oral health and implicit or explicit assessments of the necessity of dental care for people's health, the ability of many people to bear the costs themselves, and the fact that risks are reasonably predictable when people properly care for their teeth and regularly see their dentist and dental hygienist [25].

2.6 Link with the Chapters to Follow

The arrows in Fig. 2.1 correspond to the chapters to follow, although there will always be some overlap between chapters. Chapter 3 focuses on the vertical arrow that relates societal values, structures, and institutions to the design of the health system. Chapter 4 discusses the horizontal arrow from the health system design to inequalities in population health. Both these chapters look at macro-level relationships. The next chapter analyses the relationships between health system design (macro level) and health service provision (meso level). Chapter 6 covers the lower part of Fig. 2.1. It looks into the relationships between health service provision (at the meso level), the micro-level determinants of the interaction between health care providers and users, and differential service utilisation and its outcomes. How differential service utilisation and outcomes can be transformed to explain inequalities in population health (the vertical upward pointing arrow in Fig. 2.1) is covered by Chap. 7. In this chapter, we also deal with feedback loops and changes over time. This chapter completes the circle, necessary to explain why there is a macro-level relationship between the structure of health care systems and inequalities in population health. Finally, Chap. 8 wraps up the main results of the previous chapters and comes back to our second aim by discussing the added value of combining the three research areas and proposes a research agenda. This chapter brings us also back to the silos between the three research areas and how we can overcome them.

2.7 Conclusions

- We analyse the relations between health systems, health services, and population health inequalities through pathways via three levels: macro (health systems and population health inequalities), meso (health service provision), and micro (health service utilisation).

- The way the health care system is designed and funded influences the way health care providers are organised. This may restrict the options people have to use health care.
- The step from individual health outcomes to the macro level of population health inequalities is not a simple aggregation step but may require more sophisticated methods.
- We also have to take feedback loops into account. Feedback loops may change the behaviour of and interaction between health care providers and patients, and they may change the health system.

References

1. OECD. Health at a Glance 2023: OECD Indicators. Paris: OECD Publishing; 2023.
2. WHO. Closing the gap in a generation: Health equity through action on the social determinants of health. Commission on Social Determinants of Health. Geneva: World Health Organisation; 2008.
3. Wilkinson R, Pickett K. The spirit level: why more equal societies almost always do better. London: Allen Lane; 2009.
4. Marmot M. Universal health coverage and social determinants of health. Lancet. 2013;382:1227–8.
5. McCartney G, Hearty W, Arnot J, Popham F, Cumbers A, McMaster R. Impact of political economy on population health: A systematic review of reviews. Am J Public Health. 2019;109(6)
6. Coleman JS. The foundations of social theory. Cambridge, MA: Belknap Press of Harvard University Press; 1990.
7. Raub W, Buskens V, Van Assen MALM. Introduction: micro-macro links and microfoundations in sociology. J Math Sociol. 2011;35:2–25.
8. Papanicolas I, Rajan D, Karanikolos M, Soucat A, Figueras J, editors. Health system performance assessment: a framework for policy analysis. Geneva: World Health Organization; 2022.
9. Katikreddi SV, Lal S, Carrol ED, Niedzwiedz CL, Khunti K, Dundas R, et al. Unequal impact of the COVID-19 crisis on minority ethnic groups: a framework for understanding and addressing inequalities. J Epidemiol Community Health. 2021;75:970–4.
10. Greenhalg J, Manzano A. Understanding 'context' in realist evaluation and synthesis. Int J Soc Res Methodol. 2022;25(5):583–95.
11. WHO. Social determinants of health [Available from: https://www.who.int/health-topics/social-determinants-of-health
12. Fisher M, Townsend B, Harris P, Schram A, Baum F. Determinants of health: overview. In: Detels R, Abdool Karim Q, Baum F, Li L, Leyland AH, editors. Oxford Textbook of Global Public Health. 7th ed. Oxford: Oxford University Press; 2021.
13. Graham H. Social determinants and their unequal distribution: clarifying policy understandings. Milbank Q. 2004;82:101–24.
14. Marmot M, Friel S, Bell R, Houweling TAJ, Taylor S. Closing the gap in a generation: health equity through action on the social determinants of health. Lancet. 2008;372:1661–9.
15. Boudon R. The logic of social action: An introduction to sociological analysis. Boston: Routledge & Kegan Paul; 1981.
16. Mor-Anavy S, Lev-Ari S, Levin-Zamir D. Health Literacy, Primary Care Health Care Providers, and Communication. Health Lit Res Pract. 2021;5(3):e194–200.
17. Berwick DM, James B, Coye MJ. Connections between quality measurement and improvement. Med Care. 2003;41:I-30-I-8.

18. Sagan A, Thomson S. Voluntary health insurance in Europe: role and regulation. European Observatory on Health Systems and Policies. Copenhagen: WHO; 2016.
19. Keskimäki I, Tynkkynen LK, Reissell E, Koivusalo M, Syrjä V, Vuorenkoski L, et al. Finland: Health system review. Health Syst Transit. 2019;21(2):1–166.
20. Burström B, Burström K, Nilsson G, Tomson G, Whitehead M, Winblad U. Equity aspects of the Primary Health Care Choice Reform in Sweden – a scoping review. Int J Equity Health. 2017;16:29.
21. Manderbacka K, Arffman M, Lumme S, Keskimäki I. Are there socioeconomic differences in outcomes of coronary revascularisations – A register-based cohort study. Eur J Pub Health. 2015;25(6):984–9.
22. Bambra C. Cash versus services: 'worlds of welfare' and the decommodication of cash benefits and health care services. J Soc Policy. 2005;34(2):195–213.
23. Saltman R, Teperi J. Health reform in Finland: current proposals and unresolved challenges. Health Econ Policy Law. 2016;11:303–19.
24. Marrée JTC, Groenewegen PP. Back to Bismarck: Eastern European Health Care Systems in Transition. Aldershot/Brookfield USA/Hong Kong/Singapore/Sydney: Avebury; 1997.
25. Winkelmann J, Gómez Rossi J, van Ginneken E. Oral health care in Europe: Financing, access and provision. Health Syst Transit. 2022;24(2):1–169.

Open Access This chapter is licensed under the terms of the Creative Commons Attribution 4.0 International License (http://creativecommons.org/licenses/by/4.0/), which permits use, sharing, adaptation, distribution and reproduction in any medium or format, as long as you give appropriate credit to the original author(s) and the source, provide a link to the Creative Commons license and indicate if changes were made.

The images or other third party material in this chapter are included in the chapter's Creative Commons license, unless indicated otherwise in a credit line to the material. If material is not included in the chapter's Creative Commons license and your intended use is not permitted by statutory regulation or exceeds the permitted use, you will need to obtain permission directly from the copyright holder.

Chapter 3
Societal Values, Structures, and Institutions, and Their Impact on Health System Design

3.1 Introduction

In this chapter, we address the question how health care systems are influenced by the broader societal context. Broadly speaking, there are two main types of health systems research. The first poses questions about the characteristics and development over time of health systems; the health system is the dependent variable. Research into the 'social determinants' of health systems—the relationships between societal values, structures, and institutions and the characteristics of health systems—fits into this strain of research. We deal with this in this chapter. The second main strain of health systems research is about the relationships between health system characteristics, on the one hand, and population health inequalities at macro level (Chap. 4) and the provision of health services at meso level (Chap. 5), on the other hand.

In this chapter, we discuss the main similarities and differences between health systems, as shown in attempts to construct typologies of health systems. Health systems are part of the wider system of protection of citizens from catastrophes beyond their own influence, such as illness, unemployment, etc. To some extent, this wider welfare system and the health system coincide in terms of its design, but there are also countries where the principles behind the health system and the protection against loss of income due to unemployment and old age are different. We will discuss the core characteristics of health systems, and we will go into implicit and explicit priorities set in health systems.

We start by filling in the first part of Fig. 2.1, focussing on the relationships between societal values, structures, and institutions, on the one hand, and the health care system design, on the other hand, or in other words: the 'social determinants' of health care systems (see Fig. 3.1). How health care systems are organised is in the words of Sidel and Sidel [1] 'a reflection of the society's political, social, economic, and cultural history'.

Inequality in the field of health care, both in accessibility and outcomes, holds a special position in societal values. While wide disparities are accepted in other areas

© The Author(s) 2026
P. P. Groenewegen et al., *Health Systems, Health Services and Inequality in Population Health*, SpringerBriefs in Public Health,
https://doi.org/10.1007/978-3-032-02565-4_3

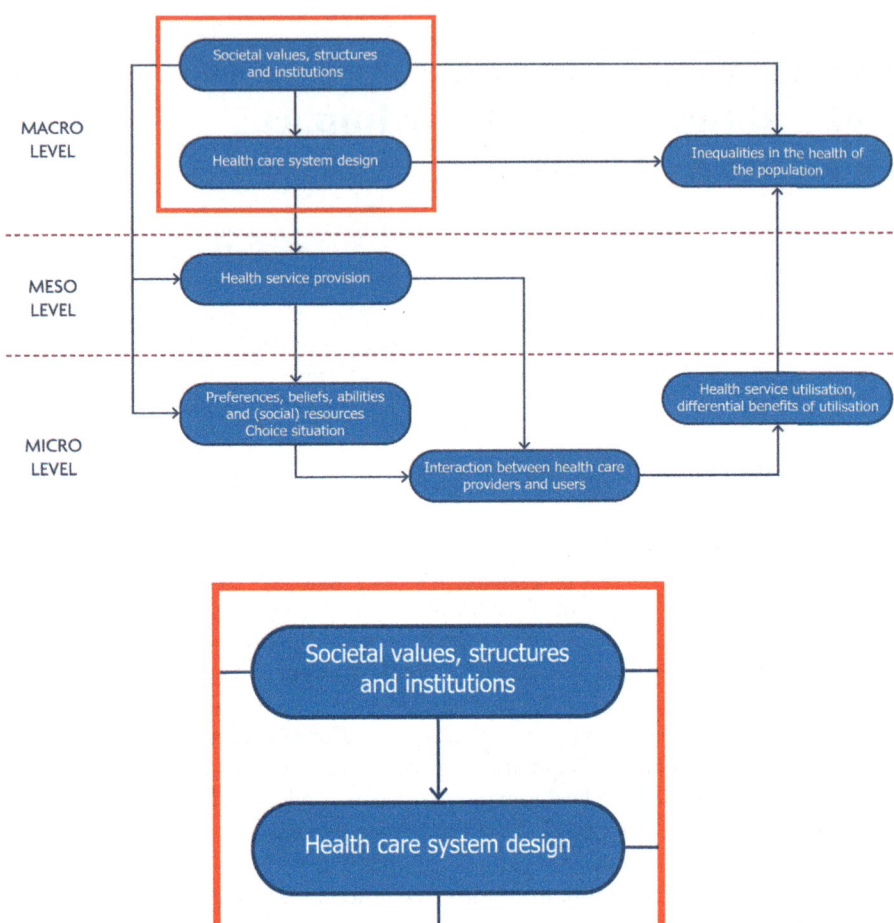

Fig. 3.1 Subsection of Fig. 2.1, highlighting the focus of this chapter

of society, such as the distribution of property, income, or education, reduction of inequalities in health care after taking differences in need into account usually appears in some form as a prime objective in health policy documents [2]. Equality in health and care also has broad support among the citizens of many countries, and differences across population groups in access to or use and quality of health services are usually morally disapproved of [3]. Accordingly, policy objectives in health systems tend to underline equality principles (which is not to say that effective policies are implemented). However, how equality goals are defined in each health system varies according to values and societal ideologies prevalent in the society in question. To illustrate these differing positions on equality in health care, Williams [4] described the two ideological grounds for health systems and policies in typical western, industrialised countries. The first ideological approach combines libertarian and the so-called desert theories of justice. 'Desert' here refers to what people deserve, according to institutional reward systems [5]. In these approaches 'access to health care is part of the society's reward system, and [...] people should be able to use their income and wealth to get more or better health care than their fellow citizens should they so wish'. Regarding the provision of health care, this type of position would best be accomplished in a market-orientated, private system with a guaranteed minimum level of health care for the population. The second ideological approach distinguished by Williams [4] sees access to health care as every citizen's right, which should not be influenced by income or wealth, but only determined by need. This would be best realised in a publicly governed system. These are ideal types and actual health care systems show a mix of these ideological positions.

3.2 Types of Health Systems

Four main types of health care systems were distinguished in the past:
- Social health insurance systems, with Germany as an example
- National health service systems, such as the NHS in the United Kingdom
- The health care system as it was in the Soviet Union and its satellite states before the resolution of the Soviet Union and
- Private health care systems, such as in the United States

With the introduction of market elements in the organisation of health care since the 1980s, as a reaction to failing planning, and later the fall of communism, the boundaries between these types became blurred and hybrid systems emerged. More recent attempts at building health system typologies start from a more systematic and empirical (rather than historical) approach, distinguishing relevant dimensions of the structure of health systems. They lead to more different types of health systems and partial membership of health systems in more than one type [6]. Partial membership means that a health system could fall under one type because of certain characteristics but under another type because of other characteristics. In this development, we could see a move from (ideal) types to the characterisation of actual health systems.

Historically, the design of health systems is part of policy diffusion processes of the original attempts to organise health care in a systemic way. Often the start of these processes is placed at the introduction of social health insurance (SHI)—the first main type of health system that we discuss here—by chancellor Bismarck in Prussia in the second part of the nineteenth century [7]. However, long before this, in many European countries, mutual support organisations developed to help each other in case of illness and work incapacity in the guilds of the Middle Ages. Although focused on mutual solidarity, these initiatives were restricted to in-groups with the exclusion of all who were outside the particular guild. The difference with SHI systems is that the latter were more universal in their coverage, although still restricted to workers and not covering all people in need of health care and income support. The long-term development of SHI systems of health care is towards broader coverage in terms of the people included and of the benefits in the insurance basket [8, 9]. The exclusion of people who do not belong to the insured population poses a risk of health inequalities. SHI was taken over and adapted in other European countries.

National health (NH) systems, funded by general taxation and often with publicly owned facilities and service providers employed by public authorities, were the alternative to organise a solidary health system. By their nature—in particular funding through taxation—NH systems are more universal in their coverage than SHI systems: all citizens are included. From an equality viewpoint, they are more inclusive than SHI systems. The first NH system originated in the UK right after the Second World War under Lord Beveridge. NH systems were also taken over by other countries, e.g. by Italy.

The third main type of health system in the past was the Soviet health system (also named Semashko system, after Nikolai Semashko [10]). Although starting from an ideology of equality, the system developed into parallel systems for elite groups in society, the military, and people working in important economic sectors, leading to inequalities in access and treatment (see Box 3.1 for more examples of parallel health care systems). The diffusion of this system structure to the Soviet republics and other countries in the Soviet sphere of influence was more a matter of coercion than of a choice by countries themselves than was the case with the diffusion of SHI and NH systems. Major health reforms, such as system changes, often take place during disruptive periods. Former Soviet republics and satellites that later joined the European Union shifted towards SHI after the fall of communism. The legal regulation of the SHI system in the Netherlands took place during World War II in a decree on sickness funds by the German occupier. The direction of change, towards NH or SHI systems, depends on dominant ideas in the period that changes are considered. For example, countries that reformed their health system in the 1960s and the 1970s tended to shift towards NH systems.

> **Box 3.1 Parallel health care systems within the mainstream health system**
> In some health care systems, parts of the population are allowed to use services provided outside the main health system. There are the so-called parallel systems of service provision. The organisation of health care in the former Soviet Union was a case in point. In many countries, there is a separate system for people serving in the army, with health care professionals as part of the military and with military hospitals. In the United States of America (USA), there is a large organisation of care for veterans, the Veterans Health Administration. Parallel systems can both aim at reducing inequalities and have increased inequality as an intended or unintended effect. The Veterans Health Administration in the USA stands out as an organisation that provides integrated care and is less inequitable than many other health systems in the USA [11].
>
> An example of a parallel system that increases health inequality is the prison health care system in most countries. Formally, prison health care is guided by the principle of equivalence, i.e. care for prisoners should be equivalent to the care that people outside prison receive. In practice, health services are less accessible to detainees and sometimes not independent of the prison organisation [12]. An example of a parallel system that seems to ameliorate health
>
> *(continued)*

Box 3.1 (continued)
inequalities is aboriginal health care in Australia. From 1971 onwards, aboriginal community-controlled health care organisations have developed. Their aim is to improve the health and health care situation of aboriginal people and their communities. Evaluations indicate that they contribute to health equality ([13]; NACCHO—National Aboriginal Community Controlled Health Organisation [14]).

Of the European countries, Finland has a large parallel system for primary care. Employed people can use the occupational health care system to use primary care services (although the exact benefits differ between employers), while people outside the workforce use the municipal health services [15, 16]. The municipal health centres have small out-of-pocket costs but long waiting times for a consultation. The occupational health care has no out-of-pocket costs, broad service coverage (but varying between employers), and short waiting times. In the figure below, a horizontal equity scale is used ranging from +1 (favouring higher income groups) to −1 (favouring lower income groups). Occupational health care favours high income groups, but to a somewhat decreasing extent from 1987 to 2014 (see Fig. 3.2). This was due to the gradually increasing coverage of doctors' clinical services in occupational health care. Municipal health centre visits are more often made by lower income people (without a trend over time).

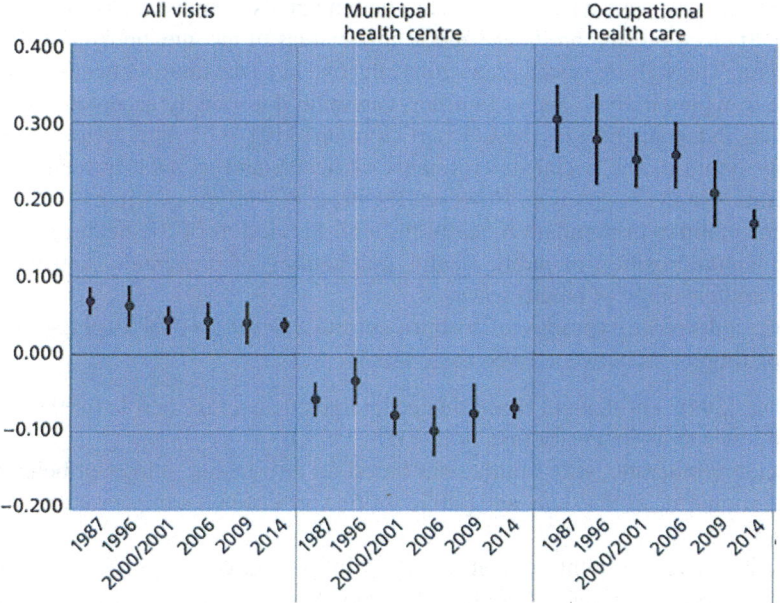

Fig. 3.2 Inequalities in doctor visits in the Finnish parallel health care system from 1987 to 2014, measured by inequity indices and 95% confidence intervals. Source: [15]. © Finnish Institute for Health and Welfare. All Rights Reserved

For some time, these three main types, supplemented by largely private health care systems as a fourth type, of which Switzerland was often seen as the European example and the USA as the main example outside Europe, formed the most used typology of health care systems [17].

The fall of communism changed the health system landscape of Europe with post-communist countries moving to SHI systems and a focus on primary care [18]. The newly formed independent states that aspired membership of the European Union had to conform to rules in several areas that also affected their health systems. Former Soviet republics that stayed outside the EU changed less and still show remnants of the Semashko system. This is, for example, visible in multispecialty policlinics and health care provision in rural areas by the so-called feldshers ('barefoot doctors'). The NH systems that were introduced in Southern Europe in the 1970s differed from their British example in a coexistence of public, NH system structures and private provision. In the Nordic countries, a vital issue in terms of NH system development was strong local communities, historically based on state church parishes. Welfare systems were rooted in these communities. It was a logical path-dependent decision to build health systems on the municipalities when other welfare functions were already run by them.

3.3 Health Systems and Broader Welfare Systems

The health system can be seen as part of the broader welfare system, which not only protects citizens against the hazards of ill health but also against unemployment and old age (pensions), and provides support in the areas of income, housing, childcare, and so on. The welfare system determines the extent of decommodification, i.e. 'the degree to which individuals, or families, can uphold a socially acceptable standard of living independently of market participation' [19] [p. 37]. The areas of support directly relate to the social determinants of health and as such influence health inequalities in the population. However, the broader welfare system may also influence inequalities in population health through the design of the health system, in particular the position of public health and funding of prevention, and universal access and coverage of health services.

The well-known typology of welfare systems, developed by Esping-Andersen [19], distinguishes between three basic types:

- Liberal, with entitlement based on need, targeted coverage, a role for the market, and low service intensity (examples: UK, USA).
- Social-democratic, with entitlement based on citizenship, universal benefits, an important role of the state, and public service provision (examples are the Nordic countries).
- Conservative, with entitlement based on insurance, coverage via employment, and a role for families (examples: Germany, Italy).

This typology was developed, based on data from the 1980s, i.e., before the fall of communism, and on a selection of 18 member states of the Organisation for

Economic Cooperation and Development (OECD). This excludes many countries, and the characteristics of the welfare systems may have changed over time as well (as have the health systems). Since its publication, the typology has been widely criticised [20], but at an abstract level it still reflects core dimensions of ideal-type welfare states. Although this typology shows overlap with the basic types of health systems, the provision of health services is not an integral part of it [21]. Bambra has added indicators for the extent to which health services can be used independent of people's (labour) market position ('decommodification'): private health expenditure, private hospital beds, and population coverage. The results show that the nature of the broader welfare system does not necessarily coincide with the nature of the health system. A case in point is the combination of a liberal welfare system and an egalitarian health system in the UK [21]. Countries with a similar type of welfare system may have a different type of health system; for example, France and Italy with conservative welfare systems, but a social insurance-based health system in France and an NH system in Italy [22].

The brief overview in this and the previous section illustrates Sidel and Sidel's [1] observation of health care systems as 'a reflection of the society's political, social, economic, and cultural history'. Emerging policy paradigms from the second half of the 1970s about the relationship between markets and the state [23, 24], the introduction of market elements in health care organisation [25], elements of New Public Management [26], the purchaser–provider split in NH systems [27], and competition between health insurance organisations in SHI systems [28, 29] all illustrate this, and they are related to reforms of health systems, with—ultimately—consequences for inequalities in health. Consequently, real-world health systems do not follow ideal types but may comprise elements of different ideal types and have service sectors operating on different principles.

3.4 Core Characteristics of Health Systems

The core elements of the structure of health care systems are identified in different ways in the literature, but they boil down to three groups that may stand in a hierarchical order, depending on disciplinary backgrounds of researchers (policy scientists, economists, …), the research focus, or theoretical approaches. For us, it suffices to note that the structural elements are interdependent, influencing each other in ways that differ between countries and health systems and that change over time. In the end, the core elements relate to: [30, 31]

- Regulation—Stewardship (relationship to other government spending, protection of certain categories of the population, vision and future orientation), governance (including relationships between sectors of health care, e.g., primary and secondary care, somatic care and mental care, health care and social care), and oversight (information to monitor the system).
- Financing—Sources of funding (taxes, insurance, and out-of-pocket payments), transfers between population categories according to age, income, health

(through pooling of insurance premiums or tax systems), and the flow of money to health care provision (ownership, contracting, and market relationships).
- Resources—Human resources (training, occupational structure in health care) and physical resources (investments in services and their management).

In relation to inequalities, regulation is important as this influences the policies and policy directions in a health system. Financing is important as it influences the fair distribution of contributions through the breadth of the benefit package and income related taxation or insurance premiums (coverage of the population). Resources, in particular how well primary care—as the first point of access—is developed, determines access to and quality of health care [32–34]. A specific aspect of access is the acceptability of service provision by (groups in) the population and the responsiveness of professionals to people's needs and preferences [30, 35, 36].

Health care regulation can roughly be allocated to the state, to markets, or to associations (professional groups, employer and employee representatives in corporate systems). This already implies consequences for the role of health systems in guaranteeing or improving equality. In general, governance through markets requires much additional regulation by the state to avoid inequalities. The emphasis on equality in health care regulation and policy differs between countries and health systems [37]. Government participation of left-wing parties is related to more policy attention to improving equality and population health outcomes. This is also the case in tax-based national health systems. Moreover, the policy attention to reducing inequalities has increased over time since the early 2000s. Mackenbach and McKee [38] analysed health policies, largely in the area of prevention, directed towards health behaviours and to health care performance (such as screening). They found that policy performance in 42 European countries is related to government effectiveness, the wealth of countries, and self-expression values in the population. In contrast to Tenbensel et al. [37], they did not find an effect of recent left-wing government participation. However, cumulated years of left-wing government participation seem to be related to effective prevention policies, suggesting that the effect was stronger in the 1970s and the 1980s and weaker afterwards [39, 40]. Effective prevention policies may in turn contribute to less health inequality.

Fair systems of financing protect people against catastrophic expenses for health care and collect money for the health system in a progressive way, i.e. wealthier people contribute more. Note that the starting point of SHI systems was the protection against poverty, with health insurance as a way of protecting workers against income loss. Financial protection against catastrophic health care expenses is roughly organised in three ways (or combinations of these). Firstly, through taxation (in NH systems); secondly, through insurance premiums (as in SHI systems) and finally, through private insurance premiums or direct payments (as in private health care systems). Underlying values for NH systems relate to equality: equal access to services for everybody according to need; for SHI systems, the underlying value is solidarity: access to services for everybody belonging to the membership of the SHI organisation; and for private healthcare systems, the underlying value is the principle of equivalence: access to service depending on ability to pay [41][Table 2.3; p. 17]. It should be noted that these underlying values have been deduced from the nature of these basic health system types; they are not based on an independent empirical study that relates values in the population of a country to the characteristics of health system. The latter would be very difficult, given the historical nature and path dependence of the development of health systems. For more recent and current reforms, a link to population values might be made empirically.

The largest flow of finances in health systems goes to hospital care; a smaller part goes to primary care and much less to prevention and public health. This partly reflects cost differences in diagnosing and treating patients with conditions that require hospital and specialist care to those that can be diagnosed and treated in primary care. At the same time, also patients are treated in hospital and by specialists that could as well or better be treated in ambulatory and primary care. As such, it reflects the priorities set in health systems. High-income countries spent 42% of total health expenditure on primary care in 2019. The share of primary care spending is higher in low- and middle-income countries: 65% in low-income countries, 58% in lower middle-income countries, and 46% in upper middle-income countries (2019) [42].

The movement towards universal health coverage (UHC) underlines the importance of access to care for everybody and aims to improve equality in service utilisation according to need, in quality of the services used, and in financial protection when in need of and using services [43, 44] (see Box 3.2). UHC emphasises the importance of access to good quality, affordable health care and not only for included population groups, as in some systems of SHI [44]. Inequality in insurance coverage is related to politics, as shown in an analysis of states in the US: better coverage in states ruled by Democrats [45]. However, it has also been noted that the contribution of UHC to equality in population health is relatively small and that it is therefore important not to lose sight of the social determinants of health [46]. On the other hand, it is difficult to think that equality in health could be achieved without health care operating more or less on the principles of UHC and providing access to health services based primarily on need.

> **Box 3.2 Universal Health Coverage**
> One of the Sustainable Development Goals (SDG) is to reach universal health coverage (UHC). It has two subgoals: SDG indicator 3.8.1 relates to service coverage and 3.8.2 to the population exposed to financial hardship due to out-of-pocket expenses. The service coverage dimension of UHC is expressed as an index based on 14 separate indicators in the field of [1] reproductive, maternal, newborn and child health, [2] infectious diseases, [3] non-communicable diseases, and [4] service capacity. UHC varies between health systems and is an important determinant of equality in access to care and ultimately in health.
>
> There has been a trend towards an increase of service coverage since 2000, indicating more equality between countries; however, this trend has attenuated since 2015.

(continued)

> **Box 3.2 (continued)**
>
> Although service coverage is highest among high income countries, there are also differences between these countries. This is not visible in Fig. 3.3, because they are all above 80 points on the coverage index. For example, countries like Iceland, Germany, and Belgium are at the higher end and Cyprus, Denmark, and Ireland at the lower end of the distribution among the countries with a service covergage index of 80 points or more.

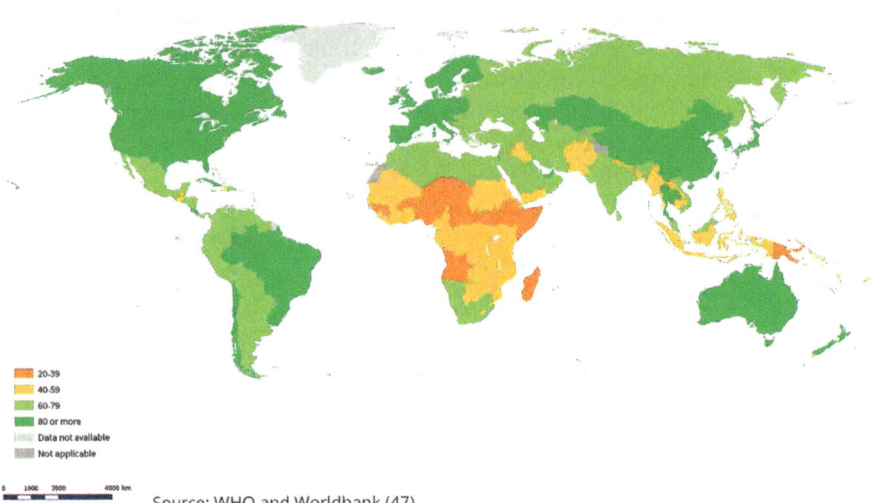

Source: WHO and Worldbank (47)

Fig. 3.3 Universal Health Coverage by country in 2021. Source: [47] (Reproduced from WHO 2023, Figure 1.5, p. 8. *Note*: This map has been produced by WHO. The boundaries, colours, or other designations or denominations used in the map and the publication do not imply, on the part of the World Bank or WHO, any opinion or judgement on the legal status of any country, territory, city, or area or of its authorities, or any endorsement or acceptance of such boundaries or frontiers. Source: WHO global service coverage database, May 2023. https://www.who.int/publications/i/item/9789240080379, licensed under the terms of the Creative Commons Attribution-NonCommercial-ShareAlike 3.0 IGO licence (CC BY-NC-SA 3.0 IGO; https://creativecommons.org/licenses/by-nc-sa/3.0/igo). Used with permission.)

How well primary care is developed is related to the wealth of countries, societal values, and political colour of governments [49]. Political influences on health systems have been discussed for a long time. The focus was largely on the influence of left-wing parties. Strong primary care is not something that develops autonomously and by itself; rather it requires deliberate policies to regulate the health care system, e.g. by introducing institutions such as gatekeeping [48]. Both the long process of strengthening primary care and the time lags in affecting population health equity require consistent policies over a longer time period. As it turns out, countries with a longer history of left-wing government participation have better developed primary care systems. They may be more willing to invest in pro-primary care policies and in measures that favour equity. The empirical research on which this is based generalises over particularities of the political situations in different countries and the interests of political parties and their constituencies. For example, left-wing parties may not be interested in the situation in rural areas where their constituency is smaller, but other parties may take this up. For instance, in Finland, the Central Party—a former agrarian party—supported universalistic social insurance and health services due to the fact that employment-based financing of health services would have left its main supporters, small-scale farmers, outside coverage as being entrepreneurs [50].

In the current political context, the possible influence of right-wing populist parties on health care and inequalities in health is important. Falkenbach and Scott characterise populist radical right-wing (PRR) parties as nativist (own people first), authoritarian, and preferring common sense above elitist knowledge [51]. In particular, the emphasis on common sense knowledge may threaten expert knowledge and professional autonomy in health care, which can be a pathway for the influence of PRR parties on health care and health [52]. This may also partly explain PRR-parties' position during the COVID-19 pandemic and on vaccinations. The no-vax movement in Italy was supported by one of Italy's PRR parties [52]. The nativist position of PRR parties may lead to exclusion policies of homeless and/or undocumented people. It extends to their position towards the EU and their international orientation in general. During the 2010–2012 government coalition supported by the PRR Party for Freedom (PVV) in the Netherlands, in particular international activities of the Ministry of Health were under pressure: 'we only bring to other countries and don't get anything back'.

The vote for PRR-parties has increased during the past decades in Europe, although government participation of these parties is in most countries still small and not yet over long periods. However, also in opposition these parties influence mainstream political parties [53]. Effects on health depend on whether health or health care is in the priorities of PRR-parties. A potential effect on equality could be restrictions on access to care for population groups that are not seen as 'native', such as (legal) immigrants. This may threaten universal health coverage [52]. In countries where PRR-parties have participated in government, their influence seems to have been through restricting access to welfare services [51]. As there is not much evidence on a direct relationship between PRR government participation and (inequalities in) health, Rinaldi and Bekker [54] focus their review of the literature on the influence on welfare policies, which is an indirect determinant of inequalities in population health. An alternative to international comparative studies is studies on local policies and the influence of local representation of PPR-parties. A study of this kind in Sweden showed less aid to vulnerable immigrants [54]. All in all, the empirical evidence of the influence of PRR-parties' government participation is still scarce. This may change in the future.

Societal values play a role in how strong primary care is. These values relate to how people look at the role of the state and of the individual, at the role of the family in taking care for older people, and at the contribution of science and technology to people's health. Empirical analysis with data from the late 1990s [49] showed that support for pro-state values coincides with stronger primary care which might be reflected in and change with political party preferences. Stronger family values were associated with weaker primary care. It is tempting to assume a very simple mechanism here: if people are willing to care for their relatives, they are less in need of primary care; however, although this could apply to home care and elderly care, it is difficult to see a direct relationship to primary care. Most probably, it has to do with broader value systems, of which family values are part as well as other values, such as those related to the role of the state. This again is linked to the welfare systems of countries, as we saw in Sect. 3.3.

The relationship of support for science and technology values with primary care—based on the same data [49]—depends on the type of health care system (no relationship in the former communist countries) and the aspect of primary care studied (positive with comprehensiveness of primary care and negative with accessibility). Richer countries had weaker primary care systems; however, behind the overall correlation are differences between countries. For example, in former communist countries, the wealth of the country and increase in wealth over time are positively related to accessibility of primary care.

3.5 Priorities in Health Systems

Societal values may not only reflect in the design of the health system but also affect priorities that are (implicitly or explicitly) placed on aspects or sectors of health care, such as health promotion and prevention or mental health care. Many priorities are implicitly set and influenced by prejudice and stigma. This may influence equality when the prevalence of stigmatised health conditions, such as mental health problems, is unequally spread over the population.

Financial flows are a first indication of priorities, as we saw in the previous section. Priorities become clear in crisis situations, when quick decisions have to be made. The COVID-19 pandemic showed the (implicit) priority placed on hospital care over long-term care and home care [55, 56]. The distribution of personal protective equipment is a case in point. Institutions that advise about guidelines and the inclusion of new treatments in the benefit package, such as NICE in the UK and Zorginstituut Nederland in the Netherlands, may prioritise areas or sectors of health care for which they review evidence and develop guidelines and how they include considerations of equity in doing so. Although it is recognised that the introduction of new therapies and how they are administered may have a disparate effect on health outcomes in different population groups, their inclusion in the benefits package of health care systems is not usually evaluated in terms of their impacts on different social groups. NICE mentions in its strategy document 'to drive the uptake of effective and cost-effective new treatments and interventions to benefit the population as a whole, and to improve and ensure equity of access to all members of society' [57]. Zorginstituut Nederland, with advising about the health insurance benefits package as one of their remits, mentions that 'reducing inequalities in health between people' [58] (p. 13; authors translation) can be one of the goals in deciding about the benefits package. However, in addition to the technical evaluation of treatments and the content of benefit packages, it may also be of importance by whom and how the decisions on the principles of service provisions are made. The general public may value reducing inequalities in health higher compared to clinicians who may have a more 'technocratic' view on health gains and value more the maximisation of health [59]. The decisions on health system designs and service provision are seldom considered openly, weighting health policy and equality goals against other issues. Economic and business interests or bigoted prejudices may influence more the decisions on developing health services than ethical deliberations.

3.6 Conclusions

- The development of health care systems follows a process of policy diffusion and reflects the society's values, economy, and politics at decisive points in time and thus is also influenced by the structural determinants of health.
- Welfare and health care system ideologies vary from people caring for themselves, people caring for each other, and the state caring for people.
- National health systems consider health care as every citizen's right and value equity for everybody. Social health insurance systems focus on the right of those insured with a potential exclusion of those who are—for whatever reasons—not insured. Private health care systems rely on market elements, and private insurance and payments.
- Core elements in the design of health systems are regulation, financing, and human and physical resources. All three have the potential to influence equality.
- In most health care systems, hospital care is the largest sector in terms of expenditure, reflecting implicit priorities.
- Government participation by left-wing political parties is related to the development of strong primary care and to more equitable health care systems.
- The effects of populist right-wing political parties lack empirical evidence but is a research priority for the future.

References

1. Sidel VW, Sidel R, Sidel VW, Sidel R. Primary health care in relation to socio-political structure. Soc Sci Med. 1977;11:415–9.
2. Van Doorslaer EKA, Wagstaff A. Equity in the delivery of health care: Some international comparisons. J Health Econ. 1992;11:389–411.
3. Whitehead M. The concepts and principles of equity and health. Copenhagen; 1990. Contract No.: EUR/ICP/RPD 414
4. Williams A. Equity in health care: the role of ideology. In: Van Doorslaer EKA, Wagstaff A, Rutten F, editors. Equity in the Finance and delivery of health care: An international perspective. Comission of the European Communities Health Services Research Series 8. Oxford: Oxford University Press; 1993.

5. Scheffler S. Justice and desert in liberal theory. Calif Law Rev. 2000;88(3):965–90.
6. Reibling N, Ariaans M, Wendt C. Worlds of healthcare: A healthcare system typology of OECD countries. Health Policy. 2019;123:611–20.
7. Busse R, Blümel M, Knieps F, Bärnighausen T. Statutory health insurance in Germany: a health system shaped by 135 years of solidarity, self-governance, and competition. Lancet. 2017;390(10097):882–97.
8. Blanpain J, Delesie L, Nys H. National health insurance and health resources: the European experience. Cambridge: Harvard University Press; 1978.
9. Busse R, Schreyögg J, Gericke C. Analyzing changes in health financing arrangements in high-income countries: A comprehensive framework approach. Washington, DC: World Bank; 2007.
10. Wikipedia. Nikolai Semashko [Available from: Nikolai Semashko (medicine).
11. NASEM. Achieving whole health: a new approach for veterans and the nation. Washington, DC: National Academies Press; 2023.
12. WHO. The WHO Prison Health Framework: a framework for assessment of prison health system performance. Copenhagen: WHO Regional Office for Europe; 2021.
13. Pearson O, Schwartzkopff K, Dawson A, Hagger C, Karagi A, Davy C, et al. Aboriginal community controlled health organisations address health equity through action on the social determinants of health of Aboriginal and Torres Strait Islander peoples in Australia. BMC Public Health. 2020;20:1859.
14. NACCHO. National Aboriginal Community Controlled Health Organisation [Available from: https://www.naccho.org.au/about-us/
15. Manderbacka K, Arffman M, Aalto AM, Muuri A, Kestilä L, Häkkinen U. Eriarvoisuus somaattisten terveyspalvelujen saatavuudessa. Suomalaisten hyvinvointi; 2018. p. 207–15.
16. Holster T, Nguyen L, Häkkinen U. The role of occupational healthcare in ambulatory healthcare in Finland. Nordic. J Health Econ. 2022;10(1)special issue.
17. Hurst J. The reform of health care: A comparative analysis of seven health OECD-countries. Paris: OECD; 1992.
18. Marrée JTC, Groenewegen PP. Back to Bismarck: Eastern European Health Care Systems in Transition. Aldershot/Brookfield USA/Hong Kong/Singapore/Sydney: Avebury; 1997.
19. Esping-Andersen G. The three worlds of welfare capitalism. London: Polity Press; 1990.
20. Bambra C. Going beyond The three worlds of welfare capitalism: regime theory and public health research. J Epidemiol Community Health. 2007;61:1098–102.
21. Bambra C. Worlds of welfare and the health care discrepancy. Social Policy and Society. 2005;4(1):31–41.
22. Ebbinghaus B. Comparing welfare state regimes: Are typologies an ideal or realistic strategy? European Social Policy Analysis Network, ESPAnet Conference; Edinburgh; 2012.
23. Saltman RB. Balancing state and market in health system reform. Eur J Pub Health. 1997;7:119–20.
24. Bartlett W, Roberts JA, Le Grand J. The development of quasi-markets in the 1990s. In: Bartlett W, Roberts JA, Le Grand J, editors. A revolution in social policy: quasi-market reforms in the 1990s. Bristol: The Policy Press; 1998. p. 1–16.
25. Saltman R, Figueras J. European health care reform: analysis of current strategies. Copenhagen: World Health Organization; 1997.
26. Noordegraaf M. Public management: performace, professionalism and politics. Palgrave Macmillan; 2015.
27. Tynkkynen LK, Keskimäki I, Lehto J. Purchaser–provider splits in health care—The case of Finland. Health Policy. 2013;111(3):221–5.
28. Greß S, Braun B, Groenewegen PP, Kerssens JJ. Consumer choice of sickness funds in regulated competition: evidence from Germany and the Netherlands. Bremen: ZeS-Arbeitspapier; 2001.
29. Maarse H, Jeurissen P, Ruwaard D. Results of the market-oriented reform in the Netherlands: a review. Health Economics Policy and Law. 2016;11(2):161–78.

30. Murray CJL, Frenk J. World Health Report 2000: a step towards evidence-based health policy. Lancet. 2001;357:1698–700.
31. Wendt C, Frisina L, Rothgang H. Healthcare system types: a conceptual framework for comparison. Soc Policy Adm. 2009;43(1):70–90.
32. Starfield B. Pathways of influence on equity in health. Soc Sci Med. 2007;64:1355–62.
33. Starfield B, Macinko J, Shi L. Contribution of primary care to health systems and health. Milbank Q. 2005;83(3):457–502.
34. WHO. World Health Report 2008 Primary Health Care. Geneva: WHO; 2008.
35. WHO. World Health Report 2000: Health systems: improving performance. Geneva: WHO; 2000.
36. WHO. WHO global strategy on people-centred and integrated health services; Interim report. Geneva: World Health Organization; 2015.
37. Tenbensel T, Eagle S, Ashton T. Comparing health policy agendas across eleven high income countries: islands of difference in a sea of similarity. Health Policy. 2012;106 (2012) 29–36.
38. Mackenbach J, McKee M. A comparative analysis of health policy performance in 43 European countries. Eur J Pub Health. 2013;23(2):195–344.
39. Mackenbach J, McKee M. Social-democratic government and health policy in Europe: a quantitative analysis. Int J Health Serv. 2013;43(3):389–413.
40. Falkenbach M, Bekker M, Greer SL. Do parties make a difference? A review of partisan effects on health and the welfare state. Eur J Pub Health. 2019;30(4):673–82.
41. Rothgang H. Conceptual framework of the study. In: Rothgang H, Cacace M, Frisina L, Grimmeisen S, Schmid A, Wendt C, editors. The state and healthcare: comparing OECD countries. Basingstoke: Palgrave Macmillan; 2010.
42. Hou X, Liu L, Cain J. Can higher spending on primary healthcare mitigate the impact of ageing and non-communicable diseases on health expenditure? BMJ Glob Health. 2022;7:e010513.
43. WHO. Health systems financing: The path to universal coverage. Geneva: World Health Organisation; 2010.
44. Kutzin J. Health financing for universal coverage and health system performance: concepts and implications for policy. Bull World Health Organ. 2013;91:602–11.
45. Zhu L, Clark JH. "Rights without Access": The Political Context of Inequality in Health Care Coverage in the U.S. States. State Polit Policy Q. 2015;15(2):239–62.
46. Marmot M. Universal health coverage and social determinants of health. Lancet. 2013;382:1227–8.
47. WHO. Tracking universal health coverage: 2023 global monitoring report. Geneva: World Health Organization and International Bank for Reconstruction and Development/The World Bank; 2023.
48. Groenewegen PP, Dixon J, Boerma WGW. The regulatory environment of general practice: an international perspective. In: Saltman RB, Busse R, Mossialos E, editors. Regulating entrepreneurial behaviour in European health care systems. Buckingham: Open University Press; 2002. p. 200–14.
49. Kringos DS, Boerma WGW, Bourgueil Y, Cartier T, Dedeu T, Hasvold T, et al. The strength of primary care in Europe: an international comparative study. Br J Gen Pract. 2013:63(e742–750).
50. Kangas O. The politics of social rights. Studies on the dimensions of sickness insurance in OECD countries. Stockholm: Swedish Institute for Social Research,1991.
51. Falkenbach M, Greer SL. Political parties matter: the impact of the populist radical right on health. Eur J Pub Health. 2018;28:15–8.
52. Pavolini E, Kuhlman E, Agartan T, Burau V, Mannion R, Speed E. Healthcare governance, professions and populism: Is there arelationship? An explorative comparison of five European countries. Health Policy. 2018;122:1140–8.
53. Falkenbach M, Greer SL, editors. The populist radical right and health: national policies and global trends. Springer Nature: Cham; 2021.

54. Rinaldi C, Bekker MPM. A scoping review of populist radical right parties' influence on welfare policy and its implications for population health in Europe. Int J Health Policy Manag. 2021;10(3):141–51.
55. Langins M, Curry N, Lorenz-Dant K, Comas-Herrera A, Rajan S. The COVID-19 pandemic and long-term care: what can we learn from the first wave about how to protect care homes? Eurohealth. 2020;26(2)
56. OVV. Aanpak coronacrisis. Deel 1: tot september 2020. Den Haag: Onderzoeksraad voor de Veiligheid; 2022.
57. NICE. NICE strategy 2021 to 2026: Dynamic, Collaborative, Excellent. London: National Institute for Health and Care Excellence; 2021.
58. ZiN. Pakketadvies in de praktijk. Wikken en wegen voor een rechtvaardig pakket. Diemen: Zorginstituut Nederland; 2017.
59. Tsuchiya A, Dolan P. Do NHS clinicians and members of the public share the same views about reducing inequalities in health? Soc Sci Med. 2007;64:2499–503.

Open Access This chapter is licensed under the terms of the Creative Commons Attribution 4.0 International License (http://creativecommons.org/licenses/by/4.0/), which permits use, sharing, adaptation, distribution and reproduction in any medium or format, as long as you give appropriate credit to the original author(s) and the source, provide a link to the Creative Commons license and indicate if changes were made.

The images or other third party material in this chapter are included in the chapter's Creative Commons license, unless indicated otherwise in a credit line to the material. If material is not included in the chapter's Creative Commons license and your intended use is not permitted by statutory regulation or exceeds the permitted use, you will need to obtain permission directly from the copyright holder.

Chapter 4
Health System Design and Inequalities in Population Health

4.1 Introduction

In this chapter, we ask ourselves the question whether there is a relationship between health system design and inequalities in population health. In research terms, the health system is the independent variable, meaning that the health system is hypothesised to influence the outcome, being inequalities in population health. This represents the second main strain of health systems research. The pathways between health system design and inequalities in population health run via the provision (meso level) and utilisation of health services (micro level), the subjects of Chap. 5 and 6, respectively.

In Fig. 2.1, we have drawn an arrow between the design of the health system and inequalities in health at population (macro) level. This relationship may be partly caused by the effects of societal values, structures, and institutions that affect both the distribution of health in the population and the design of the health system through social determinants of health and system design (see Fig. 4.1). The health system design, in its turn, affects individual health outcomes through pathways of service provision and utilisation and the transformation of these outcomes to population level. In this chapter, we discuss the links between health care system design and inequalities in health.

The direct relationship between the design of the health care system and inequalities in population health is an ecological relation at macro level. There are several drawbacks to the empirical analysis of ecological relationships. In particular when we have health systems or countries as the units, the numbers are usually small, often not more than 20. This means that we do not have enough observations to take other characteristics of health systems or countries into account, with the risk that we attribute a relationship to the health system while it is actually a consequence of another characteristic that relates both to characteristics of the health system and

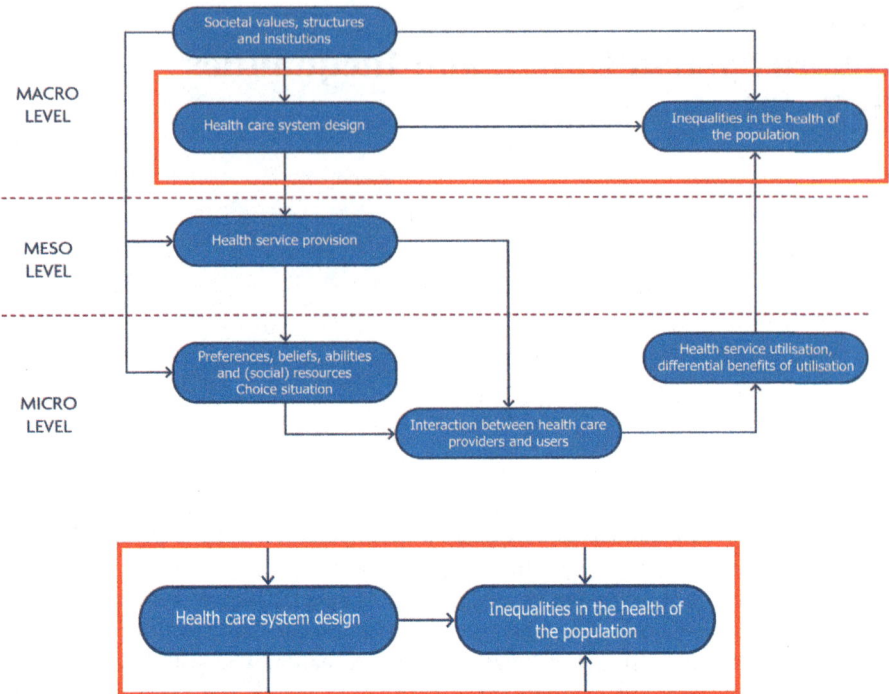

Fig. 4.1 Subsection of Fig. 2.1, highlighting the focus of this chapter

inequalities in population health. The second drawback is that in an ecological analysis, we do not test the pathway between the health system and inequalities in population health which run via meso and micro level, but nevertheless often make inferences about the pathways. This is known as an ecological fallacy, where a pathway via meso or micro level is wrongly assumed (and not tested) [1]. An example could be that a relationship between cost-sharing in health care and inequalities in population health is attributed to patients delaying to seek care or not seeking care, while it could also be the case that the explanation has to be sought in how health care providers treat patients from lower socioeconomic groups.

The extent to which inequalities in population health exist is one of the performance areas of health systems, indicating the importance of reducing inequalities as an aim of health policy in many countries. Several frameworks for the analysis of health system performance (Health System Performance Analysis or HSPA) have been developed by separate countries and by international organisations, such as the World Health Organisation (WHO) and the Organisation for Economic Cooperation and Development (OECD). In HSPA, equality is an important area, as shown in an overview of frameworks for HSPA [2]$^{(Table\ 2.3)}$. It is often mentioned, but less often operationalised in measurable indicators [3]. If so, the focus is perhaps more on process indicators (such as access) than outcome indicators (such as socioeconomic differences in health). The WHO performance framework, underlying the World Health Report 2000 'Health systems—improving performance', has a clear focus on equality in its characterisation of the three main goals of health systems: improving population health and its distribution, responsiveness to the needs and preferences of patients/citizens, and the fairness of financial contributions [4]. On the national level, the Belgian health system performance analysis has published a separate report on inequalities [5]. It covers inequality in health care use, unmet needs, and equality in health care expenditure and financing, and shows, for example, large differences between educational and income categories in use of dental care.

4.2 The Contribution of Health Care to Population Health and Inequalities

Over time, the influence of health care on population health has increased, in particular in high-income countries [6, 7]. Therefore, the potential to address health inequalities through health care may also have increased. Access to effective health care and the provision of health services with an eye on inequalities are important policy areas that require inputs from health systems research as well as health services research. The responsibility of health care for social determinants of health inequalities is gradually increasing and this is a result of policies and not of autonomous changes. With the (long-term) change of morbidity from infectious disease to chronic disease, prevention has to move from infection prevention and vaccination to programmes to support people in changing their lifestyle. This in itself exposes the relationships between health care and health inequalities, as those interventions that require a contribution from individuals tend to increase inequalities rather than reduce them. People lacking resources (e.g. in terms of time, money, or education) and abilities are less often reached by and will find it harder to participate in lifestyle prevention programmes.

The increased impact of health care on population health is related to a combination of the coverage of more effective treatments and services in the benefits packages of health systems, and increased quality and better organisation of care. One may think of the introduction of effective (drug) treatment in the form antibiotics against infectious diseases, secondary prevention of lifestyle-related diseases, and organisation of care for stroke in dedicated stroke units. The contribution of health care to population health has been analysed by Johan Mackenbach in his book *'A History of Population Health: Rise and Fall of Disease in Europe'* [6]. Part of the epidemiological transition from mortality caused by infectious disease to morbidity caused by lifestyle-related diseases is the availability of effective treatment for infectious diseases. Estimates for the Netherlands show that half of the increase in life expectancy at birth in the period 1950–2000 resulted from better medical care for infectious disease. Although there might also be an increased impact of health care on inequalities in population health, the evidence is scarce, and the trend is not necessarily towards more equality.

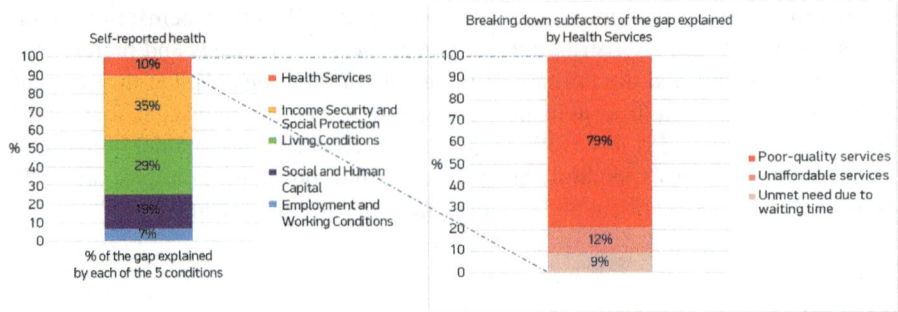

Fig. 4.2 Health systems and services' contributions to inequalities in self-reported health in European Union member states. Source: Reproduced from WHO 2019 [8], Figure 0.11 (source: WHO authors' own compilation based on data extracted for the years 2003–2016 from the EQLS). https://iris.who.int/handle/10665/326879, licensed under the terms of the Creative Commons Attribution-NonCommercial-ShareAlike 3.0 IGO (CC BY-NC-SA 3.0 IGO) licence (https://creativecommons.org/licenses/by-nc-sa/3.0/igo). Used with permission

An analysis for WHO European Region [8] estimates the contribution of health systems and services to inequalities in health. Ten percent of the inequalities in self-reported health and 11% of the inequalities in mental health are attributable to health systems and services as shown in Fig. 4.2. The left-hand side of this figure also shows the continuing importance of social determinants of health.

This analysis was based on large population surveys and restricted to indicators of self-reported health as outcomes. Other indicators of health would include morbidity as presented to and assessed by health care providers and mortality, in particular avoidable mortality, i.e. mortality that can be avoided by timely application of good quality care. The analysis in this report does not attempt to relate the differences between countries or health systems to characteristics of the health systems. However, the attribution of inequalities in health to the contribution of health services clearly motivates the link to health system design. A systematic review of the impact of the political economy on population health cites improving the coverage and reducing out-of-pocket payments as policies to address inequalities [9]. This underscores the importance of the movement towards universal health coverage (see Chap. 3, Sect. 3.6 and Box 3.1).

4.3 Health Expenditures and Inequalities in Population Health

Apart from specific characteristics of health systems, health care expenditures are related to inequalities in mortality [7]. In an analysis of European countries, inequality in all-cause mortality was lower in countries that spend more on health care [10]. That this relationship is not straightforward is illustrated by the much-discussed position of the United States of America (USA) in terms of health expenditures and population health outcomes and equity [11]. Higher expenditures in OECD member states are related to longer life expectancy and better population health outcomes in two out of five indicators (life expectancy and maternal mortality) [12]. A higher level of social expenditure compared to health expenditures is related to better outcomes in terms of life expectancy, infant mortality, and fewer potential years of life lost, but at the same time a higher incidence of low birth weight. However, in these international comparisons, specific indicators on equality are often lacking.

Health outcomes for specific medical conditions and services show a stronger relationship with health care expenditure. However, there seems to have been a widening of relative differences in mortality due to conditions amenable to medical care for people from different occupational classes in England and Wales in the period from the 1930s to the 1960s. This is at least to some extent due to differential benefits from better (access to) medical treatment (see also Chap. 6) [13]. In contrast, in Scotland, between 2000 and 2010, a 43% fall in mortality from coronary heart disease was observed. This fall could be evenly attributed to improvements in treatments (health services) and in risk factors (through health promotion), with little evidence of socioeconomic patterning in either change [14]. This is remarkable in the light of previous research that suggested that primary prevention of cardiovascular disease among high-risk people rather increased socioeconomic differentials in health [15].

4.4 Complexity and Fragmentation of Health Systems

A rather general characteristic of health systems is how complex they are for patients to navigate. Finding their way in the insurance system and its benefits may be difficult for citizens and once they become patients, navigating the system may also be difficult. Whether people are able to cope effectively with the health system depends on their personal resources and social networks. Health systems differ in how complex they are. While health care providers may approach this by saying that patients differ in how complex their health problems are, Dionne Kringos, in a presentation about primary care, once remarked: 'there are no complex patients, only complex health systems'.

It may be hypothesised that regarding coverage and benefits, health systems are more complex if coverage depends on insurance that people have to take out themselves, if there are many different insurance policies, and if benefits are not in-kind and depend on authorisation. The complexity of the health system has been connected to inequalities as this title of a recent editorial shows: Complexity in the US health system is the enemy of access and affordability [16]. There is a body of literature on what is called health insurance literacy. This concept relates to the abilities of people to make the right choices in taking out insurance and choosing between different policies. The concept has (not surprisingly) been developed in the USA and also been applied in the Netherlands, where people have to choose between many different policies [17, 18]. Health insurance literacy is lower in older people and those with lower education [18], pointing to inequality effects as a result of a choice for an insurance policy that does not match people's needs.

The complexity of health systems for people with multiple diseases (multimorbidity) is well known. It may be hypothesised that this is more the case if care is less integrated, if information exchange between different care providers is less well organised, and if there is no single care provider to coordinate care. Hospitals are still mostly organised in silos along medical specialities, without much coordination, making patients (and their family or informal carers) to become the coordinator of their own care. In some health systems, the idea of a patient navigator has been developed. Navigators are often volunteer-lay persons with more extended knowledge about the care system. Again, this concept has been developed in the USA but also applied in other countries [19]. People may be able to cope with the complexities of the health system better when they are more health literate. Health literacy, again, is related to people's personal resources, such as education, and their social networks. People with lower health literacy have worse health outcomes compared to those with more health literacy [20]. The effect may be stronger, the more complex the health systems is. However, it is unclear whether this is a result of social determinants influencing both health literacy and health, or a result of differential access and utilisation of care.

4.5 Market Elements in Health Systems

Changes in health systems and their influence on inequalities in population health are important in documenting the influence of health system characteristics on inequalities. They provide opportunities for research designs to analyse natural experiments (see Chap. 7). Changes in many health systems in Europe during the past two decades are in the direction of incorporating elements of competition among health care providers, insurance organisations and purchasers of care, and of New Public Management [21]. These changes, often summarised as market reforms in health care, do not necessarily evolve towards meeting the changing population health needs. Depending on the incentives incorporated in these changes, they may have led to the emergence of inequalities in population health [9, 22]. Health care providers do not work where needs are biggest, but where the incentives of the system, such as fee-for-service payments, are strongest. In the 1970s, John Tudor Hart neatly summarised this in the inverse care law: care is less available where needs are biggest [23].

A recent development is the emergence of private equity (What's in a name?) firms in health care that buy health care facilities with an eye to increasing shareholder value, often with negative effects on patients, health care staff, and neighbouring facilities [24]. This is an example of the broader issue of commercial determinants of health and health care. The commercial determinants of health (CDoH), defined as 'the systems, practices and pathways through which commercial actors drive health and equity', both positive and negative, have received attention during the past years [25]. They include such direct influences on health as smoking, alcohol consumption, and diet. Commercial influences on health care receive less attention; however, a recent overview of commercial determinants of noncommunicable (chronic) diseases by WHO also gives attention to commercial determinants of health care and describes the role of private equity and of the pharmaceutical and medical devices industries [26]. CDoH are related to health inequality, for example, by focusing advertisements to vulnerable groups in society. Commercial determinants of health care may also be related to equality through direct-to-consumer marketing of pharmaceutical products. This is not allowed in the European Union, but the Internet provides enough opportunities to bypass. Also pricing practices may affect equality [26].

The emergence of private equity firms shows that international financial flows and trade (e.g. in pharmaceuticals) have become more important. The focus on the health systems of nation states may increasingly become too restrictive in the analysis of health systems in relation to equality as a result of the importance of border-crossing flows of money, pharmaceuticals, and devices. Studies of networks of countries and health systems may be a solution.

4.6 Primary Care and Equality

Primary care is an important part of health system design. If people have a long-standing relationship with a primary care provider, they may receive support in the management of their disease and in navigating the complexities of the health system. As a consequence, primary care is often seen as a means to address inequalities in health. Despite the fact that this often hypothesised, there are a few studies that directly relate characteristics of primary care to inequality in population health. Barbara Starfield initiated a number of studies, investigating the correlates of strong primary care, both in ecological studies within the USA and between countries. A review of these studies pointed to a moderating effect of better primary care on the relationship between income inequality and health outcomes, in particular self-rated health. Better primary care was often indicated by the supply of primary care physicians per 100,000 population and US states or counties were used as units of analysis [27]. An example of such a study is Shi et al. who analysed 50 US states with primary care physician supply as characteristic of primary care and including two controls (total physician to population ratio and smoking prevalence). This study showed the moderating effect of primary care [28]. An interesting feature of the US studies is that federal states with differences in the characteristics of health care provide an interesting 'laboratory' for studying the impact of health care on equity, as many other historical and institutional influences are common among the states or regions within a federation. However, differences between health care systems (in the USA meaning of the term) may be more important than differences between states.

An international comparative ecological analysis showed that primary care systems with better continuity of care coincide with less inequality in self-rated health [29]. The analysis included 27 countries and was corrected for an important health behaviour, the percentage of the population who are daily smokers. It is remarkable that there are (as far as we know) no recent ecological studies into the relationships between health system characteristics and equity in health. Given the claims about the importance of primary care for equality in health [30], we would expect much more attention to the subject. Although improving equality is often stated policy—e.g., in 7 out of 21 countries in a European study in the first decade of this century—the actual implementation of policies lagged behind [31]. Salmi et al. reviewed 143 projects. The biggest category was providing health promotion in the community; the second was improving financial access to health care for low-income groups and the third was modifying health care provision. The authors found only little evidence of the effects of the projects they identified. However, specific investments in equality policies in primary care have been shown to have effects in a comparison of two different health systems, one with a general investment policy in primary care and one with an equality improvement strategy. Mortality amenable to health care fell more in the health system with specific equality policies and this was stronger in the most deprived neighbourhoods [32].

A recent review study on primary care interventions to improve equality reinforces the conclusion that the evidence base is still rather weak [33]. It is difficult to analyse equality improving interventions and policies in primary care because of the context dependence of primary care. What works in rural areas perhaps does not work in urban areas, what works in more affluent areas perhaps does not work in deprived areas, and what works in one system perhaps does not work in another system. This is why the authors of this review propose five organising principles that may facilitate equality-oriented policies and interventions in primary care:

- Design interventions as *connected components* of coordinated action (e.g. in the areas of risk assessment and screening, financial incentive schemes, and cultural sensitivity of primary care staff).
- Account for the *differences between patients* and the differential effects of services (e.g. interventions that rely on individual action or agency, such as self-management or educational interventions, often do not work for patients in deprived circumstances).
- Care delivery should be *flexible* to allow for different patient needs, preferences, and resources.
- *Inclusive* and *intersectional* policies rooted in an organisational culture of primary care that does not exclude people because of who they are, what they do, and how they should behave.
- Primary care should be *population-oriented and community-based* to allow involvement of patients, population as well as primary care staff [33].

These rather general principles of strong primary care underscore the potential of primary care in reducing inequalities in health and health care utilisation; however, what interventions are effective in doing so remains inconclusive.

As highlighted in these organising principles of equality-oriented primary care, health systems may influence equality in population health through stimulating participation or engagement of patients or citizens [34]. Health systems may mobilise intersectoral action and facilitate social empowerment and thereby influence inequalities in health. In some health care systems, public consultations are required around the introduction of large-scale changes in health care, thereby giving voice to citizens/patients; however, the reach of these consultations in terms of numbers and diversity of people who participate is low [35]. An older review of the impact of community engagement did not find effects on population health or the quality of services [36]. However, a more recent review [37] concluded that there is a positive impact on health outcomes. An impact on health equality at population level has not been reported. Hence, there is no conclusive evidence on the role of community engagement in improving service quality and decreasing inequalities in population health.

4.7 Conclusions

- Over time, the influence of health care on population health has increased and thus the potential to influence inequalities in health.
- Inequalities in population health is one of the performance areas of health care systems.
- According to an analysis for WHO Euro, 10% of the inequalities in self-reported health and 11% of the inequalities in mental health are attributable to health services.
- Higher health expenditures and lower out-of-pocket expenses relate to more equality.
- The complexity and fragmentation of health systems make it difficult to navigate the systems for people with less resources and abilities.
- Changes in health care systems towards more market elements may have led to inequalities in population health.
- Strong primary care system is related to less inequality in access and health outcomes, but the evidence base is still rather weak.

References

1. Diez Roux AV. Bringing context back into epidemiology: variables and fallacies in multilevel analysis. Am J Public Health. 1998;88:216–22.
2. Papanicolas I, Rajan D, Karanikolos M, Soucat A, Figueras J, editors. Health system performance assessment: a framework for policy analysis. Geneva; 2022.
3. Lee-Foon NK, Haldane V, Brown A. Saying and doing are different things: a scoping review on how health equity is conceptualized when considering healthcare system performance. Int J Equity Health. 2023;22:133.

4. Murray CJL, Frenk J. A framework for assessing the performance of health systems. Bull World Health Organ. 2000;78(6):717–31.
5. Bouckaert N, Maertens de Noordhout C, Van de Voorde C. Health System Performance Assessment: how equitable is the Belgian health system? Brussels: Belgian Health Care Knowledge Centre (KCE); 2020.
6. Mackenbach J. A history of population health: Rise and fall of disease in Europe. Leiden: Brill/Rodopi; 2019.
7. Nolte E, McKee M, Evans D, Karanikolos M. Saving lives? The contribution of health care to population health. In: Figueras J, McKee M, editors. Health systems, health, wealth and societal well-being: Assessing the case for investing in health systems. Maidenhead: Open University Press; 2012.
8. WHO. Healthy, prosperous lives for all: the European Health Equity Status Report. Copenhagen: World Health Organisation Regional Office for Europe; 2019.
9. McCartney G, Hearty W, Arnot J, Popham F, Cumbers A, McMaster R. Impact of political economy on population health: A systematic review of reviews. Am J Public Health. 2019;109(6):e1–e12.
10. Mackenbach J, Bobb M, Deboosere P, Kovacs K, Leinsalu M, Martikainen P, et al. Determinants of the magnitude of socioeconomic inequalities in mortality: A study of 17 European countries. Health Place. 2017;47:44–53.
11. Papanicolas I, Woskie LR, Ashis K. Health care spending in the United States and other high-income countries. JAMA. 2018;319(10):1024–39.
12. Bradley EH, Elkins BR, Herrin J, Elbel B. Health and social services expenditures: associations with health outcomes. BMJ Qual Saf. 2011;20:826–31.
13. Mackenbach J, Stronks K, Kunst AE. The contribution of medical care to inequalities in health: Differences between socio-economic groups in decline of mortality from conditions amenable to medical intervention. SocScMed. 1989;29(3):369–76.
14. Hotchkiss J, Davies CA, Dundas R, Hawkins N, Jhund PS, Scholes S, et al. Explaining trends in Scottish coronary heart disease mortality between 2000 and 2010 using IMPACTSEC model: retrospective analysis using routine data. Br Med J. 2014;348:g1088.
15. Capewell S, Graham H. Will cardiovascular disease prevention widen health inequalities? PLoS Med. 2010;7(8):e1000320.
16. Levitt L, Altman D. Complexity in the US health system is the enemy of access and affordability. JAMA Health Forum. 2023;4(10):e234430.
17. Kim J, Braun B, Williams AD. Understanding health insurance literacy: A literature review. Fam Consum Sci Res J. 2013;42(1):3–13.
18. Holst L, Rademakers J, Brabers AEM, de Jong JD. The importance of choosing a health insurance policy and the ability to comprehend that choice for citizens in the Netherlands. Health Lit Res Pract. 2021;5(4):e288–e94.
19. McBrien KA, Ivers N, Barnieh L, Bailey JJ, Lorenzetti DL, Nicholas D, et al. Patient navigators for people with chronic disease: a systematic review. PLoS One. 2018;13(2):e0191980.
20. Nutbeam D, Lloyd JE. Understanding and responding to health literacy as a social determinant of health. Annu Rev Public Health. 2021;42:159–73.
21. Simonet D. The new public management theory and the reform of European health care systems: an international comparative perspective. Int J Public Admin. 2011;34(12):815–26.
22. Bambra C, Garthwaite K, Hunter D. All things being equal: Does it matter for equity how you organize and pay for health care? A review of the international evidence. Int J Health Serv. 2014;44(3):457–77.
23. Tudor HJ. The inverse care law. Lancet. 1971;297(7696):405–12.
24. Rechel B, Tille F, Groenewegen PP, Timans R, Fattore G, Rohrer-Herold K, et al. Private equity investment in Europe's primary care sector—a call for research and policy action. Eur J Pub Health. 2023;33(3):354-355.
25. Gilmore AB, Fabbri A, Baum F, Bertscher A, Bondy K, Chang H-J, et al. Defining and conceptualising the commercial determinants of health. Lancet. 2023;401(10383):1194–213.

References

26. WHO. Commercial determinants of noncommunicable diseases in the WHO European Region. Copenhagen: WHO Regional Office for Europe; 2024.
27. Starfield B, Shi L, Grover A, Macinko J. The effects of specialist supply on populations' health: assessing the evidence. Health Aff. 2005;25:W5-97-W5-107.
28. Shi L, Starfield B, Kennedy BP, Kawachi I. Income inequality, primary care, and health indicators. J Fam Pract. 1999;48:275–84.
29. Kringos DS, Boerma WGW, Van der Zee J, Groenewegen PP. Europe's strong primary care systems are linked to better population health but also to higher health spending. Health Aff. 2013;32:686–94.
30. Starfield B. Improving equity in health: a research agenda. Int J Health Serv. 2001;31(3):545–66.
31. Salmi L-R, Barsanti S, Bourgueil Y, Daponte A, Piznal E, Ménival S. Interventions addressing health inequalities in European regions: the AIR project. Health Promot Int. 2017;32:430–41.
32. Cookson R, Mondor L, Asaria M, Kringos DS, Klazinga NS, Wodchis WP. Primary care and health inequality: difference-in-difference study comparing England and Ontario. PLoS One. 2017;12(11):e0188560.
33. Gkiouleka A, Wong G, Sowden S, Bambra C, Siersbaek R, Manji S, et al. Reducing health inequalities through general practice. Lancet Public Health. 2023;8:e463–72.
34. Gilson L, Doherty J, Loewenson R, Francis V. Challenging inequity through health systems. Knowledge Network on Health Systems. Technical Report. WHO Commission on the Social Determinants of Health. Final report. 2007.
35. Djellouli N, Jones L, Barratt H, Ramsay AIG, Towndrow S, Oliver S. Involving the public in decision-making about large-scale changes to health services: a scoping review. Health Policy. 2019;123:635–45.
36. Milton B, Attree P, French B, Povall S, Whitehead M, J. P. The impact of community engagement on health and social outcomes: a systematic review. Community Dev J. 2011;47(3):316–34.
37. Haldane V, Chuah FLH, Srivastava A, Singh SR, Koh GCH, Seng CK, et al. Community participation in health services development, implementation, and evaluation: a systematic review of empowerment, health, community, and process outcomes. PLoS One. 2019;14(5):e0216112.

Open Access This chapter is licensed under the terms of the Creative Commons Attribution 4.0 International License (http://creativecommons.org/licenses/by/4.0/), which permits use, sharing, adaptation, distribution and reproduction in any medium or format, as long as you give appropriate credit to the original author(s) and the source, provide a link to the Creative Commons license and indicate if changes were made.

The images or other third party material in this chapter are included in the chapter's Creative Commons license, unless indicated otherwise in a credit line to the material. If material is not included in the chapter's Creative Commons license and your intended use is not permitted by statutory regulation or exceeds the permitted use, you will need to obtain permission directly from the copyright holder.

Chapter 5
Health System Design and Service Provision

5.1 Introduction

In this chapter, the question is how the design of health systems affects the provision of services. This is part of the pathway through which health care systems affect health inequalities. In Chap. 3, the health system design was the dependent variable, and we addressed the factors influencing the features of the health systems. Here, as in the previous chapter, the health care system design is the independent variable. We focus on its impact on service provision (see Fig. 5.1). Some issues have already been discussed in Chap. 3 and 4, such as values and priorities in health care, but they come back here with the focus on their implications for service provision.

For the purpose of this book, to analyse how service provision may lead to inequalities in health, accessibility will be used as the organising principle. Accessibility refers to the possibilities to access (and use) services. The latter, actual access and utilisation, is the subject of Chap. 6. Accessibility of health services is a multidimensional concept. Often it is considered in terms of insurance coverage or physical location of health care facilities with adequate numbers of health care professionals. However, from the point of view of people needing care, also psychological and cultural aspects are important. Based on their synthesis of literature on the conceptualisation of access to health care, Levesque et al. have designed a framework to analyse these dimensions in more detail and to take into account the demand-side features of the population and the process through which access is realised [1]. They distinguish five aspects of accessibility (Fig. 5.2): approachability, acceptability, availability, affordability, and appropriateness [1]. In general, access results in differential utilisation of services in the interaction between supply of and demand for services. This interaction is the subject of Chap. 6; here we focus on how the design of the health system influences these aspects of accessibility. This is the top part of Fig. 5.2 within the black rectangle.

© The Author(s) 2026
P. P. Groenewegen et al., *Health Systems, Health Services and Inequality in Population Health*, SpringerBriefs in Public Health,
https://doi.org/10.1007/978-3-032-02565-4_5

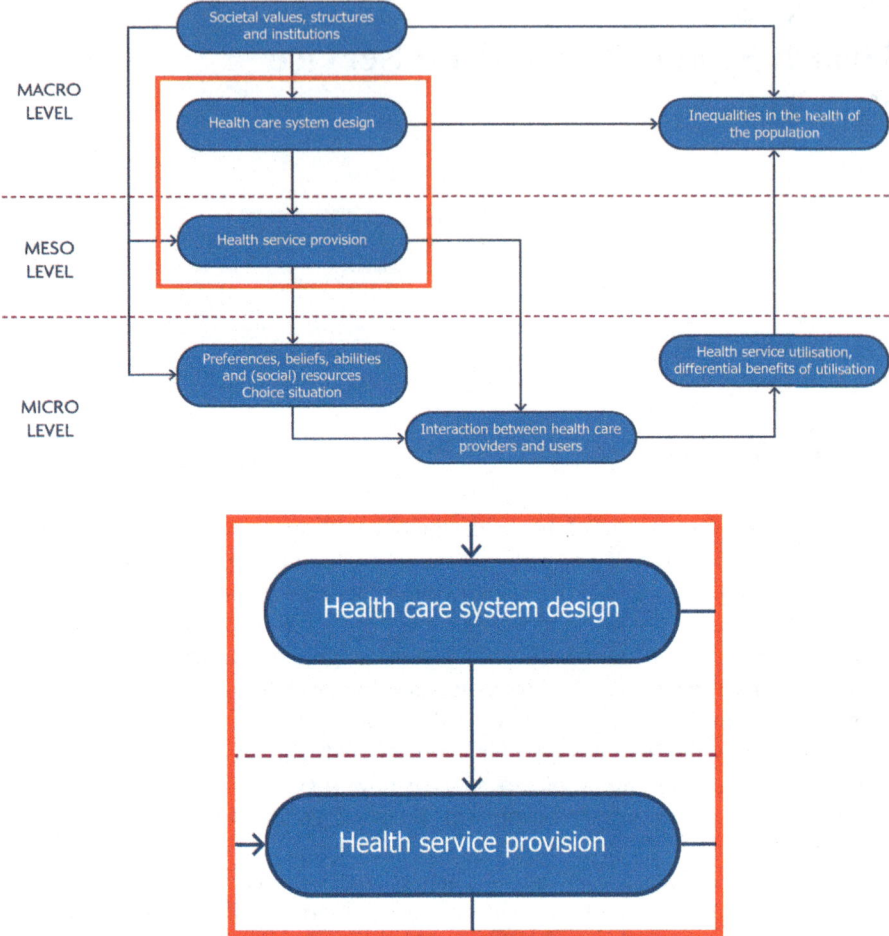

Fig. 5.1 Subsection of Fig. 2.1, highlighting the focus of this chapter

5.2 Approachability

Approachability refers to whether information is available to the population about services and how to approach them. In increasing order of activity, this relates to information, guidance, outreach activity, and active screening. In general, there is (as far as we know) a lack of research that connects health system design to approachability. However, we can think of health system characteristics that are potentially related to approachability, but this should be tested in future research.

Concerning information, publicly accessible information on local health and social care services and their characteristics, including care quality may be better available in health systems with stronger role for local authorities, such as the Nordic countries, compared to health systems with a smaller role for local

5.2 Approachability

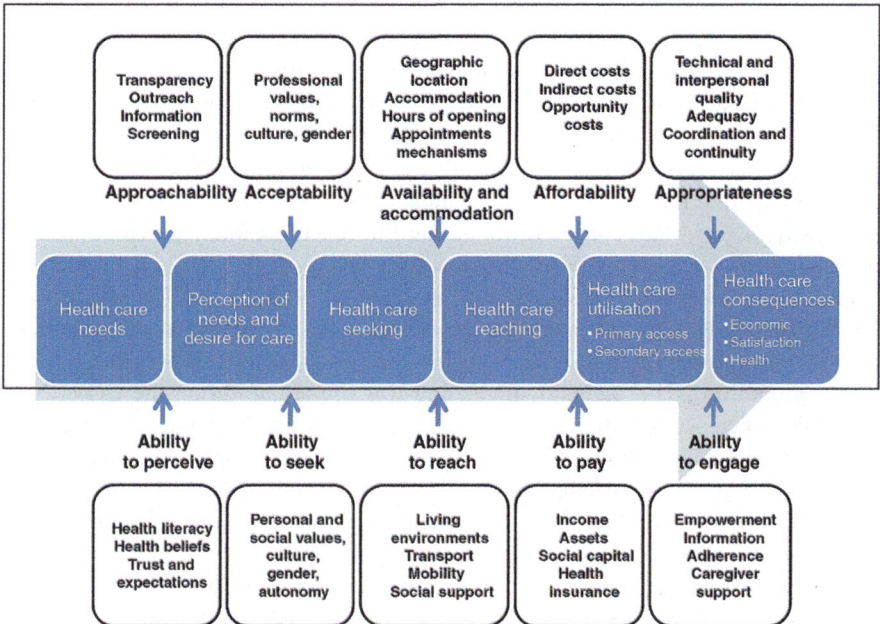

Fig. 5.2 A conceptual framework of accessibility of health care; focus on the top part. Source: Reproduced from Levesque 2013 [1], Figure 2. A minor modification was made. https://doi.org/10.1186/1475-9276-12-18, licensed under the terms of the Creative Commons Attribution License (http://creativecommons.org/licenses/by/2.0)

authorities. The health systems with a smaller role for local authorities could be both more centralised systems, such as France, or social health insurance systems, such as Germany.

Digital and online information on services provided, quality of care, and so on are increasingly available in high-income countries. From a point of view of equality in access, it is important that information is available in minority languages and for people with low health literacy. The question is whether this depends on the design of health systems or rather on more general societal structures, including the demography of countries and general attitudes towards minorities.

When people need specialist care, it is sometimes unclear where to get this care and from what speciality. Patients with multiple chronic diseases experience the fragmentation of health care and the silos of different specialisms in hospitals (see also Chap. 4, Sect. 4.4. Complexity of Health Systems). Primary care plays a role in guiding patients to the right service. Guidance is facilitated by a system of gatekeeping and perhaps by population responsibility of primary care and of hospitals. Originating in the United States of America (USA), systems with a weak primary care system have developed the idea of navigators [2]. Navigators, often volunteers, help patients finding their way in a complex health system.

Outreaching activities of health care providers are increasingly important with a growing elderly population living in the community. In the past, health care providers could be reactive—if patients do not contact a health care provider, they were assumed to be healthy; however, this assumption seems to be increasingly invalid. Actively outreaching to people above a certain age who have not been in contact with the primary care practice, e.g., during a year, is a strategy to take responsibility for the population rather than only for patients who take initiative themselves. It is also a way of providing care to different hard-to-reach populations with a lack of information or who perceive and experience care as less acceptable. An important condition for outreaching activities of health care providers is that they know who their population is. This is related to primary care providers having a defined patient list and hospitals having a responsibility for the care of a defined population, both more common in NH systems. Outreaching was important during the COVID-19 pandemic, when accessibility of primary care practices and hospitals was restricted due to infection prevention (and reluctance of patients to visit care providers). However, a study on outreaching activity of primary care practices during the pandemic did not show a relationship with having a patient list system [3]. The community orientation of primary care (awareness of the health needs of the population, assuming responsibility and involving the local community) was stronger in health systems with a list system in an international comparative study [4].

Screening—not only for cancer or communicable diseases, but also, for example, for frailty in the elderly—is also easier with a defined patient list. Screening is usually seen as a task for public health authorities; however, research shows that screening and vaccination by general practitioners (GPs) lead to a higher coverage, probably as a result of easier access and trust in GPs [5].

5.3 Acceptability

The acceptability of care to (sections of) the population is related to professional norms and values and actual behaviour of health care providers, and the experiences and perceptions of people with this. Acceptability refers to people's/patients' expectations of good, non-judgmental treatment, communication, and trust. Fear of negative reactions may refrain people from seeking care or postponement of care. More comprehensive and accessible primary care in a country is associated with less financially driven postponement of visits to primary care [6, 7]. Actual experiences of primary care patients with lower education, less income, or a migration background show less positive experience in all major areas (communication, accessibility, continuity, coordination and comprehensiveness of care, and the experience of being discriminated). First-generation migrant patients experience more discrimination in health care when visiting a native GP, compared to visiting a GP who was her/himself born elsewhere [8]. Consequently, the diversity in the health care workforce relates to the experiences of patients. However, as far as we know this is not directly related to health system characteristics; indirectly, via the influence of societal structures and values on health systems, it will be related [9].

Responsiveness or the degree to which health care provision matches the expectations varies between service providers and countries or health systems. A major attempt to document health system responsiveness was made in the WHO World Health Report 2000 on 'Health systems: improving performance' [10]. A review after 20 years since this publication showed that there still is a lack of evidence on the relationship between responsiveness to the expectations of different groups in society and equality in health [11]. Responsiveness can be facilitated by information systems on patient experiences that may provide feedback to local health service providers and national policy and decision-makers, by complaint systems, and by community participation. However, these channels are less often used by people on low income or with less education, thus reproducing existing inequality in responsiveness to their expectations. In this case, a feedback loop is missing (scenario 1 in Fig. 2.3). Health system design elements that relate to these responsiveness increasing channels consist of their institutionalisation in governance and policy [11]. Incentives for providers to behave in a responsive way may depend on payment systems, may also be countered by professional norms and standards. For example, commercial chains of GP practices in the Netherlands have tended to (implicitly and explicitly) select younger and healthier patients because of the capitation payment for each patient on the list which provides a stable income flow, while patients with more care needs, such as patients with multiple chronic diseases or patients with language problems did not receive the care they expected and moved to the list of other GPs. In general, however the cited review concludes that there is a lack of evidence about the relationship between health system design and responsiveness.

5.4 Availability and Accommodation

A major factor determining physical accessibility or availability of and the population's ability to reach services is the geographical distribution of service provision. This is influenced by decisions to allocate resources and to establish providers. Health care facilities are less available in rural and remote areas, where the population is shrinking and ageing, and younger people are moving out, e.g., to follow higher education. Consequently, this process of sorting out leads to imbalances between care supply and needs, affecting elderly people, the lower educated, those without access to means of transport, and in general more vulnerable people most [12].

Research suggests that the geographical distribution of hospital beds is influenced by politics: the distribution of hospital beds is more equal in countries/regions with a longer tradition of left-wing government participation [13, 14]. The same association was found for the physical accessibility of general practices for people with disabilities [15]. However, it is simplistic to consider disparities in access to service only in terms of one-dimensional party-political influence. It is a question about wider societal drivers and values: Which diseases are prioritised to be treated; whose health needs are considered important to meet; and which virtues of health care are valued more in decision-making: efficiency or equity? (see Box 5.1).

> **Box 5.1 Health Equality Impact of Proposed Health Facility Changes**
> Health impact analysis usually focusses on environmental policies. However, also health policies may have an impact on equality of health, e.g., by changing the accessibility of health services. Health care facilities, such as hospitals, but also primary care practices, have increased in size over the past decades. Part of this is caused by concentration of care through mergers or takeovers. Research on the consequences of mergers and takeovers concentrates on the quality of care in the newly formed organisations, compared to comparable non-merged care organisations. Accessibility is an understudied quality consequence of mergers and takeovers.
>
> In the Netherlands, mergers or takeovers of care organisations need the approval of the Dutch Care Authority if more than 50 care providers are involved. The organisations that intend to merge or do a take-over, among other things, have to provide information on whether they have taken the consequences for continuity and accessibility of care into account. A formal health equality impact analysis is not required. New York State has a law (in effect from June 2023) on the assessment of the health equality consequences of health facility changes (reduction, relocation, and closure of a part of a hospital). Uttley reports on health equality assessments that have identified the negative impact of the closure of a birth centre [16]. Black pregnant women, a vulnerable group who experience high rates of maternal mortality and morbidity, and with less access to transportation, would have more difficulty in accessing a midwife-led birth centre if the one under study would be closed.
>
> Health impact assessment is required for major construction projects or to add, expand, or reduce services. The assessment must identify the number and type of medically underserved people who would be affected by the facility's proposed project. The affected community has to be involved in the assessment procedure through surveys, community forums, or interviews with key stakeholders.

Physical accessibility is not only geographical; it also refers to the actual accessibility of the health care premises in terms of opening hours and waiting times, telephone and digital accessibility, or accessibility for people with disabilities [15]. Opening hours outside the normal office hours may be important for low-income workers who may not be able to take time off for a visit to a health care facility [17]. Waiting times tend to be longer in state-run health care systems and lower when health care providers, such as general practitioners are self-employed. People with higher education and income are often able to get quicker access because of abilities to manage their way in the system, to use their network or pay for quicker access by going private (in systems where public and private care facilities exist next to each other) or by paying under the table.

The incentives in the health care system, such as payment systems for services, influence where providers can earn an income and thus where they work. This is not necessarily where need is biggest (inverse care law; see Chap. 4, Section 4.5) [18].

5.5 Affordability

Health systems differ in the extent to which people are covered for their health care. Coverage has three dimensions (Fig. 5.3). The first dimension is how many people are covered for (part of) the costs of health care, the population coverage. Not everybody has access to insurance. Undocumented people or homeless people are not or only partly covered for their health care use in many health systems. Some countries have (e.g. Germany) or had (e.g. the Netherlands) obligatory health insurance for people below a certain income ceiling and private, voluntary insurance for those above the ceiling. The second dimension relates to which services are covered. The size of the benefits package in different countries is difficult to compare. Health systems with fee-for-service payment have service catalogues with services that can be billed and the associated amounts, but national health service systems and systems with capitation payments have less explicit definitions of the benefits basket [20]. Whether and how this affects equality in access is unclear. Finally, the third dimension is the share of the costs of health service utilisation that is covered. Whether or not people can afford to use health services depends on the direct costs of out-of-pocket payments and insurance premiums, and on indirect costs, e.g., costs of transportation (related to geographical availability) and opportunity costs (related to opening hours for working people on low-income jobs). These costs may be so high that they have catastrophic consequences for households. The World Health Organisation (WHO) has published data on catastrophic health care costs, see Box 5.2.

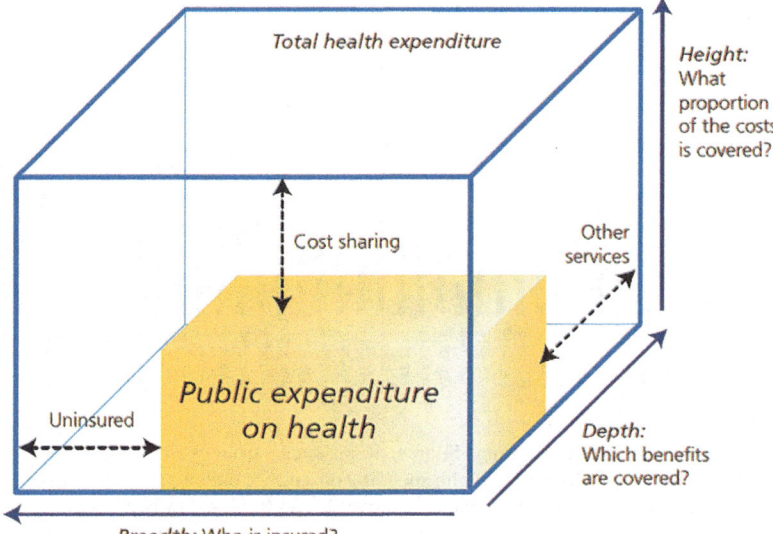

Fig. 5.3 Three dimensions of coverage decisions. Source: Reproduced from Winkelmann et al. 2018 [19], Figure 1. https://iris.who.int/handle/10665/332568, licensed under the terms of the Creative Commons Attribution-Attribution-NonCommercial-NoDerivs 3.0 (CC-BY-NC-ND 3.0) licence (https://creativecommons.org/licenses/by-nc-nd/3.0/deed.en). Reproduced with the permission of the European Observatory on Health Systems and Policies

Box 5.2 Catastrophic Health Spending

Coverage of the costs of health care is important to have a fair distribution of health care costs and to prevent households from financial hardship due to health care utilisation. Out-of-pocket payments in particular for prescription drugs are the cause of catastrophic health spending. Figure 5.4 shows that the poorest quintile in the population is hit hardest. High out-of-pocket payments lead to people refraining from use of health care with possible health consequences in the long run. WHO Europe adds five policy options that should be avoided under the chapter 'Addiction' to bad ideas. The coverage policy choices that undermine financial protection are:

1. Avoid basing entitlement on payment of contributions
2. Avoid excluding people from coverage
3. Avoid applying user charges without effective protection mechanisms
4. Avoid failing to cover treatment in primary care settings
5. Avoid thinking voluntary health insurance (VHI) is the answer.

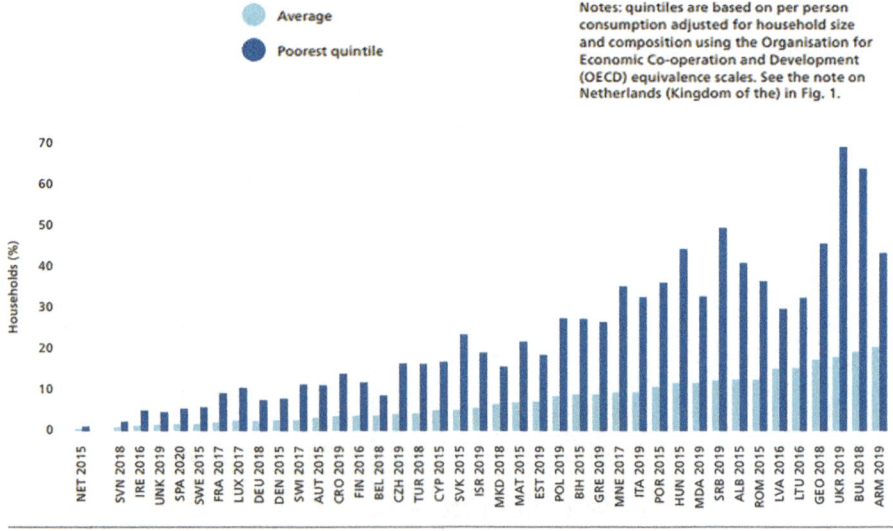

Fig. 5.4 Catastrophic health spending. Source: Reproduced from WHO 2023 [23], Figure 2. Share of households with catastrophic health spending on average and in the poorest quintile, 2019 or the latest available year before COVID-19. Source: WHO Regional Office for Europe (2023). UHC watch [online database]. Copenhagen: WHO Regional Office for Europe (https://apps.who.int/dhis2/uhcwatch/#/). Minor modification was made. https://iris.who.int/bitstream/handle/10665/374814/WHO-EURO-2023-8969-48741-72485-eng.pdf, licensed under the terms of the Creative Commons Attribution-NonCommercial-ShareAlike 3.0 IGO (CC BY-NC-SA 3.0 IGO) licence (https://creativecommons.org/licenses/by-nc-sa/3.0/igo). Used with permission

Financial accessibility or affordability and ability to pay are first related to direct costs of consultations (out-of-pocket payments, cost-sharing), the costs of getting to the facility, and the opportunity costs of not being able to do other (income-generating) activities, but second to the population's capacity to bear these costs. Evidently, these costs weigh heavier for people on lower income, and they may forego seeking care when they feel it is needed, although there may be compensation for higher costs, depending on countries' social safety net and insurance regulations. Direct, out-of-pocket payments coincide with increased inequalities in health [21].

The public–private mix of service provision influences decisions about coverage and whether or not people can afford to use health care. The public–private mix is in turn influenced by the design of health systems. In National Health (NH) systems, the public share is biggest and in market systems the private share is biggest, with social health insurance systems somewhere in between. Private provision of services is in general most common in dental care and in pharmacies [22]; however, dentists may have a contract with the NH system or with social insurance organisations, depending on the benefit basket in a country. Also, general practitioners (GPs) are often self-employed with a contract to the public system. According to Rothgang et al. [22] the public provision of health services has declined in most of the member states of the Organisation for Economic Development and Cooperation (OECD) they studied over the period 1990–2003.

5.6 Appropriateness

While acceptability (see Sect. 5.4) focussed on how potential patients view the health service providers, appropriateness focusses on the way health services are provided. Important aspects of appropriate care are that care is patient-centred, effective, and efficient. Appropriate care takes into account the needs of patients, their preferences, and their cultural values. We assume that in health systems that have regulation in place to assess and improve quality of care the chances of receiving appropriate care are higher. However, the question is whether these chances differ for people with different characteristics. In other words: is there equality in receiving appropriate care?

Choosing wisely is a movement, started in the 2010s, that tries to identify low-value or unnecessary diagnostics and treatments and to reduce their use by care providers [24]. Low-value diagnostics and treatments are an example of inappropriate care. Research in the United States shows that black and Hispanic citizens are more likely to receive low-value care [25].

Continuity of care between parts of the health care system, such as inpatient and outpatient care or somatic care and mental health care, increases the chances that appropriate care is provided. A strong primary care sector that guides patients to the right provider when they need care that cannot be provided at the primary level increases appropriate care.

Many health systems are oriented towards hospital and specialised care, both in terms of the allocation of money and the availability of human resources. Treatment is often more important than prevention; consider, for instance, preventive services (vaccinations, maternity, and childcare), occupational health services, or rehabilitation. The orientation of health systems can be gathered from their expenses, and the supply of medical specialist as compared to primary care physicians or nurses and the supply of hospital beds. The system of health accounts developed by the Organisation for Economic Cooperation and Development (OECD) has made national expenses to some extent comparable. The expenditures for 'general outpatient curative care' as percentage of total health expenditures are highest in Poland (12.4%) and lowest in Switzerland and Germany (3.8%), while the expenditures for prevention are highest in Denmark (5.2%) and low—less than 1%—in countries, such as the Netherlands, Belgium, and Luxemburg (source: OECD Health Statistics 2023). Research in the USA shows that the supply of primary care physicians at county level is related to better population health in terms of lower mortality and that no such relation is found for the supply of specialist care [26]. In the European Union, Greece is the country with the largest number of specialists but lowest number of nurses. Acute hospital bed supply is largest in Germany (5.8 beds per 1000 population) and lowest in the Netherlands (2.2 beds) in 2021 (source: OECD health data). To what extent the differences in orientation of health systems relate to equality in health is not known.

5.7 Conclusions

- Accessibility is multidimensional and affects different population groups in different ways.
- It is related to the design of health systems, but this link has seldomly been studied in international, comparative research.
- A defined population for which health care providers are responsible and strong primary care are beneficial for several aspects of accessibility.
- Availability of care providers is an important problem in remote rural areas and in private health systems also in inner city areas, leading to inequalities in access.
- Affordability of care benefits from universal health coverage in terms of population, services, and costs covered.
- There are inequalities in receiving appropriate care by ethnic groups, but there is a lack of research outside the USA.

References

1. Levesque J-F, Harris MF, Russell G. Patient-centred access to health care: conceptualising access at the interface of health systems and populations. Int J Equity Health. 2013;12:18.
2. Budde H, Williams GA, Scarpetti G, Kroezen M, Maier CB. In: Sagan A, editor. What are patient navigators and how can they improve integration of care? Copenhagen: WHO; 2022.
3. Van Poel E, Collins C, Groenewegen PP, Spreeuwenberg P, Bojaj G, Gabrani J, et al. The organization of outreach work for vulnerable patients in general practice during COVID-19: results from the cross-sectional PRICOV-19 study in 38 countries. Int J Environ Res Public Health. 2023;20:3165.
4. Vermeulen L, Schäfer W, Rotar-Pavlic D, Groenewegen PP. Community orientation of general practitioners in 34 countries. Health Policy. 2018;122(10):1070–7.
5. Tacken MAJB, Braspenning JCC, Hermens RPMG, Spreeuwenberg P, Van den Hoogen HJM, De Bakker DH, et al. Uptake of cervical cancer screening in the Netherlands is mainly influenced by women's beliefs about about the screening and by the inviting organization. Eur J Pub Health. 2007;17:178–85.
6. Detollenaere J, Van Pottelberge A, Hanssens L, Boerma WGW, Greß S, Willems S. Patients' financially driven delay of GP visits: Is it less likely to occur in stronger primary care systems? Med Care Res Rev. 2018; 75(3):292–311.
7. Detollenaere J, Hanssens L, Vyncke V, De Maeseneer J, Willems S. Do we reap what we sow? Exploring the association between the strength of European primary healthcare systems and inequity in unmet need. PLoS One. 2017;12(1):e0169274.
8. Groenewegen PP, Spreeuwenberg P, Siriwardena AN, Sirdifield C, Willems S. Migrant GPs and patients: a cross-sectional study of practice characteristics, patient experiences and migration concordance. Scand J Prim Health Care. 2022; 40(2):81–9.
9. NASEM. Ending unequal treatment: strategies to achieve equitable health care and optimal health for all. Washington, DC: The National Academies Press; 2024.
10. WHO. World Health Report 2000: Health systems: improving performance. Geneva: WHO; 2000.
11. Khan G, Kagwanja N, Whyle E, Gilson L, Molyneux S, Schaay N, et al. Health system responsiveness: a systematic evidence mapping review of the global literature. Int J Equity Health. 2021;20:112.
12. Bosmans MWG, Boerma WGW, Groenewegen PP. Imbalances in rural primary care: A scoping literature review with an emphasis on the WHO European Region. Geneva: WHO; 2021.
13. Westert GP, Groenewegen PP. Regional disparities in health care supply in eleven European countries: does politics matter? Health Policy. 1999;47:169–82.
14. Bennema-Broos M, Groenewegen PP, Westert GP. Social democratic government and spatial distribution of health care facilities: the case of hospital beds in Germany. Eur J Pub Health. 2001;11:160–5.
15. Groenewegen PP, Kroneman M, Spreeuwenberg P. Physical accessibility of primary care facilities for people with disabilities: a crosssectional survey in 31 countries. BMC Health Serv Res. 2021;21:107.
16. Uttley L. New Health Equity Impact Assessment Law in New York Beginning to Show Results. Milbank Memorial Fund; 2024 [Available from: https://www.milbank.org/2024/06/new-health-equity-impact-assessment-law-in-new-york-beginning-toshow-results/
17. Kona M, Houston M, Gooding N. The effectiveness of policies to improve primary care access for underserved populations: an assessment of the literature. Milbank Memorial Fund. 2022.
18. Tudor HJ. The inverse care law. Lancet. 1971;297(7696):405–12.
19. Winkelmann J, Panteli D, Blümel M, Busse R. Universal health coverage and the role of evidence-based approaches in benefit basket decisions. Eurohealth. 2018;24(2):34–7.

20. Busse R, Van Ginneken E, Schreyögg J, Velasco-Garrido M. Benefit baskets and tariffs. In: Wismar M, Palm W, Figueras J, Ernst K, Van Ginneken E, editors. Cross-border Health Care in the European Union: Mapping and analysing practices and policies. Observatories studies series. Copenhagen: European Observatory on Health Systems and Policies; 2011. p. 91–120.
21. Mackenbach JP, Kunst AE. Evidence for strategies to reduce socioeconomic inequalities in health in Europe. In: Figueras J, McKee M, editors. Health systems, health, wealth and societal well-being: Assessing the case for investing in health systems. Maidenhead: Open University Press; 2012.
22. Rothgang H, Cacace M, Frisina L, Schmid A. The changing public-private mix in OECD healthcare systems. In: Seeleib-Kaiser M, editor. Welfare state transformations: comparative perspectives. Houndmills & New York: Palgrave Macmillan; 2008.
23. WHO. Can people afford to pay for health care? Evidence on financial protection in 40 countries in Europe. Summary. Copenhagen; 2023.
24. Cliff BQ, Avanceña ALV, Hirth RA, Lee SD. The impact of choosing wisely interventions on low-value medical services: a systematic review. Milbank Q. 2021;99(4):1024–58.
25. Schpero WL, Morden NE, Sequist TD, Rosenthal MB, Gottlieb DJ, Colla CH. For selected services, blacks and hispanics more likely to receive low-value care than whites. Health Aff. 2017;36(6):1065–9.
26. Starfield B, Shi L, Grover A, Macinko J. The effects of specialist supply on populations' health: assessing the evidence. Health Aff. 2005;25:W5–97-W5–107.

Open Access This chapter is licensed under the terms of the Creative Commons Attribution 4.0 International License (http://creativecommons.org/licenses/by/4.0/), which permits use, sharing, adaptation, distribution and reproduction in any medium or format, as long as you give appropriate credit to the original author(s) and the source, provide a link to the Creative Commons license and indicate if changes were made.

The images or other third party material in this chapter are included in the chapter's Creative Commons license, unless indicated otherwise in a credit line to the material. If material is not included in the chapter's Creative Commons license and your intended use is not permitted by statutory regulation or exceeds the permitted use, you will need to obtain permission directly from the copyright holder.

Chapter 6
Health Service Provision and Differential Service Utilization, Treatment, and Benefits

6.1 Introduction

In this chapter, we pose the question how the provision of health services affects inequalities between social groups through differences in utilisation of services, the kind of services received, and the benefits from these services. Social groups may be defined by characteristics, such as income, education, or ethnicity. Health services provision may lead to inequalities in three steps: first, through differential utilisation (non-use, delayed use) of health services; second, through differences in the health services provided; and third, through differential effects of the services used. These three steps can be illustrated by three reports on socioeconomic differences in cancer diagnosis and care by IKNL (Integraal Kankercentrum Nederland; Netherlands Comprehensive Cancer Organisation). The first report describes differences before and around the diagnosis [1]. Many forms of cancer are more prevalent in people on a low income as a result of social determinants of health and disease. At the time of diagnosis, the stage of the cancer is less favourable for people on a low income for some cancers (such as cervical cancer, breast cancer, and prostate cancer). Part of the explanation for this is that participation in population-based screening programmes is lower for people with a lower socioeconomic status. The second report discusses differences around treatment [2]. For a number of cancers, such as breast, prostate, non-small cell lung, colon cancer, and melanoma, patients on lower income undergo (major) cancer treatment less often than patients on higher income. For example, for non-metastatic cancer, radiation is more often used instead of surgery (in the case of lung and prostate cancer) and systemic treatment is given less often. This may partly be explained by patients' lower socioeconomic status. People with lower socioeconomic status more often have comorbidities, more often a poorer condition and more often a higher BMI. They also more often have insufficient or limited health literacy and are less able and less willing to travel longer for medical oncological care. The third report treats the third step; that of the consequences of treatment in terms of survival, quality of life, work and income, and care after cancer treatment [3]. People on lower income survive less long; this difference becomes smaller the longer people survive. No difference between income categories was found in recurrence or progression of the cancer. Quality of life among people with or after cancer differs along the lines of income and education. People on higher income have less problems in the area of work; they have slightly more control visits and receive slightly more after-care. These three steps are the subject of this chapter.

In Chap. 5, we addressed the design of the health system and how its features may impact the differential or unequal use of health services. In this chapter, we step down to the individual level and scrutinize factors related to individual patients' chances of gaining access to and utilising health services, as well as benefiting from this utilisation. In terms of the framework of Fig. 2.1, the focus of this chapter is on how health service providers interact with patients (see Fig. 6.1). The meso level of the provision of health services, in combination with patients' characteristics, such as preferences, beliefs, abilities, and other (social) resources, may lead to patients' differential utilisation and potentially unequal benefits from health care use. This result may be explained by provider characteristics, such as quality of medical decision-making or prejudice in their encounters with patients on low income, with low education, or a different ethnic background.

In Chap. 5, we used the framework on access to health services presented by Levesque et al. [4], focusing on the upper part of the framework that depicts the dimensions of accessibility aligned with the structure of health systems. In this chapter, the focus shifts to the lower half of the framework, which depicts the abilities of individuals, patients, and often families to use health services. While these abilities are important, the decisive factor is the interaction between the arrangements of health care provision and health professionals, on the one hand, and patients' and their families' or carers' preferences, beliefs, abilities, and other resources, on the other hand. Although these features are individual, they are influenced by people's social circumstances. Examples of abilities are people's health literacy and their ability to navigate an increasingly complex health system (see also Chap. 4, Sect. 4.4. Complexity of Health Systems).

In terms of the benefits that the use of services renders to patients, the quality and effectiveness of services are crucial, as well as the patients' ability to benefit from the services. Hence, the functional consequences during and after treatment may differ between groups of patients. To complete the view, we also consider the impact of different health services throughout people's life histories and the process of accumulation of these impacts.

6.2 Gaining Access to Health Services

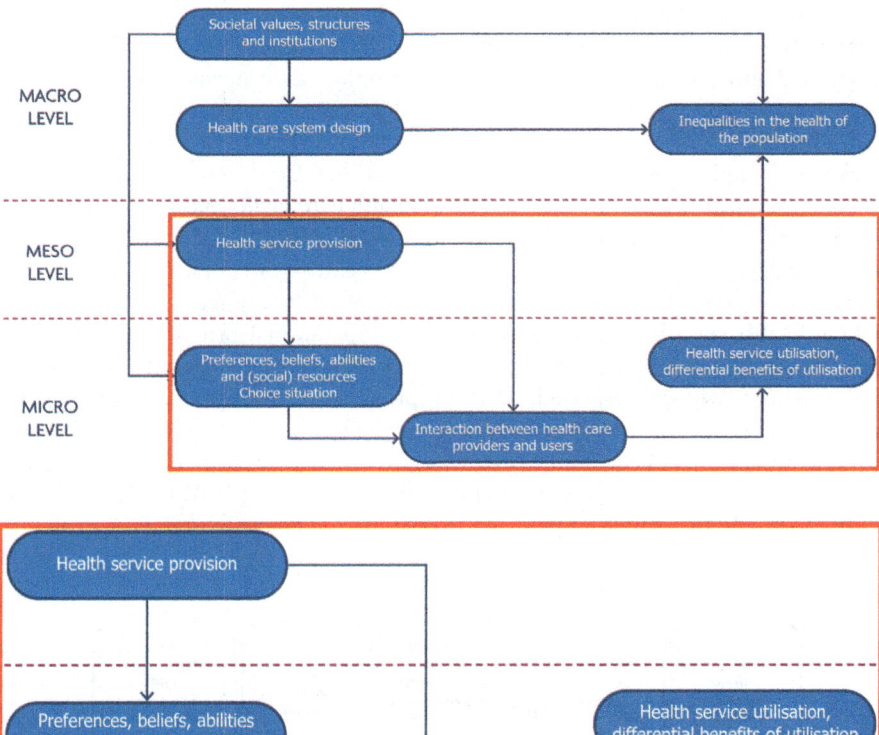

Fig. 6.1 Subsection of Fig. 2.1, highlighting the focus of this chapter

6.2 Gaining Access to Health Services

Health insurance coverage and the physical location of health care facilities with adequate numbers and skills of health care professionals do not guarantee that the need for health care is adequately met for all sub-groups of the population. While these universal arrangements of health provision are necessary for organising adequate supply of care, health services may vary in terms of content, quality, and effectiveness, and the results of this variation are often related to patients' social positions. To address these considerations, the Institute of Medicine (IOM) has defined effective access as 'the timely use of personal health services to achieve the best possible health outcomes' [5]. This definition emphasises the rationale of using health services, namely, to improve health, beyond just focusing on barriers and facilitators to gaining access to services.

As discussed in Chap. 5, factors aligned to health system design which impact accessibility operate on different dimensions. These dimensions influence actual access and utilization of care, considering people's care needs and the process through which access is realized. This chapter focuses on the lower part of Levesque et al.'s framework of access. We reproduce the figure on the framework here with a black square underscoring the topic of analysis (Fig. 6.2).

The process of realized access runs from health care needs and people's perception of these needs and their wish to use care, to actual health care utilization and its consequences. As explained in Chap. 5, on the health system or supply side, this process is influenced by five dimensions of accessibility aligned with factors such as how health systems are designed and their operational principles. These five dimensions are: (1) Approachability; (2) Acceptability; (3) Availability and accommodation; (4) Affordability; and (5) Appropriateness. The lower part of Fig. 6.2 contains the five corresponding abilities of people to interact with these health system side dimensions of accessibility to generate actual access and utilization. In the framework, these five abilities are: (1) Ability to perceive; (2) Ability to seek; (3) Ability to reach; (4) Ability to pay; and (5) Ability to engage.

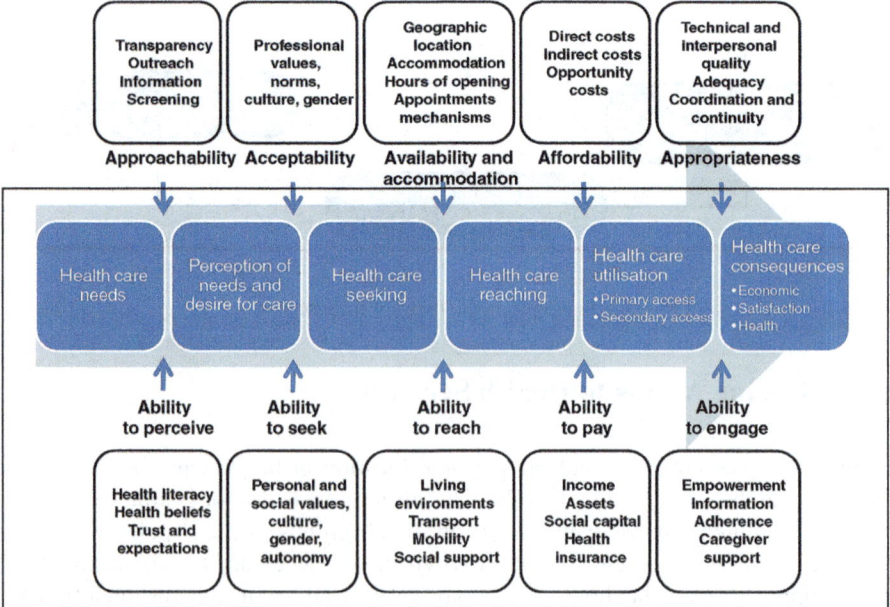

Fig. 6.2 A conceptual framework of accessibility of health care; focus on the lower part. Source: Reproduced from Levesque 2013 [4], Fig. 2. A minor modification was made. https://doi.org/10.1186/1475-9276-12-18, licensed under the terms of the Creative Commons Attribution License (http://creativecommons.org/licenses/by/2.0)

Abilities to Perceive Need and to Seek Care

Approachability and acceptability—information about the existence and availability of the service and how to reach it, and that the services are organized in a manner that the population largely accepts—are self-evidently important prerequisites for people's decisions to use health services. There are counterparts on the demand or potential patients' side, namely, abilities to perceive the need for care and to seek services.

The ability to perceive the need for care is important for the formation of a person's intentions to use health services. Awareness of having a disease is an important condition for seeking care. As an example, the Belgian Health Examination Survey showed that 10% of the population has diabetes, but that two-thirds of them is not aware of having diabetes (and hence is not treated). Undiagnosed diabetes is more prevalent among people with a lower education level [6]. The ability to perceive is strongly related to health literacy and knowledge and beliefs about health and illness, which are further influenced by social and cultural factors [7]. The inability to seek care manifests itself in unmet needs. Unmet needs are higher in lower socioeconomic groups, with lower health literacy, and they are often, but not necessarily related to the costs of using health care or the insurance status of people [8]. From these examples and from Chap. 5, it is clear that accessing health care is influenced by the combination of characteristics of health service provision and characteristics of patients. The ability to gain access to care encompasses personal autonomy and requires knowledge about health options, rights, and opportunities. A more equal distribution of this knowledge is a condition to begin receiving health services.

While the dimensions of the abilities in the framework appear to underline an individualistic notion of responsibility for health and service use, the framework actually emphasises the interplay of the dimensions of accessibility of health services and abilities of patients. Access to and use of health services take place in a social context. The decision to seek health care is taken by individuals and/or their family, with support and information from their wider social network. These decisions can be facilitated and supported by designing the system and services to lower the thresholds for use. Alternatively, health services can be organised in a way that secures the use of services for those who may have limitations in recognising health needs or seeking help. This may sound trivial and self-evident, but despite evidence on the importance of services, such as outreach services or call and recall systems, these services to support seeking care are not widely adopted in health systems. During the COVID-19 pandemic, primary care practices worked in an outreaching way in many countries by, e.g., actively addressing people with chronic conditions who did not contact the practice themselves [9]; however, it is unclear (and perhaps not to be expected) whether this was retained after the situation normalised again.

Abilities to Reach and to Pay for Care

Concrete examples of how the design of health systems and service provision impact access to and use of services and their socioeconomic patterning, are the abilities to reach and to pay for health care in the framework. In the framework by Levesque et al., the ability to reach health care refers to characteristics enabling a person to reach service providers. These characteristics include individual mobility, means of transportation, flexible work arrangements, as well as sufficient knowledge about the provision of health services. The ability to pay for health care refers to the capacity to generate economic resources to pay for health care services without excessive use of resources needed for ordinary life. In Chap. 5, we provided ample examples of how factors such as geographical locations of services, opening hours of practices, and cost-sharing and direct payments may substantially influence different population groups' possibilities to use services. While active decisions to increase direct payments in health care or to change the location of service providers may influence the social patterning of health care use, *not* making such decisions may have similar effects. For instance, an unregulated establishment of medical practices has, to some extent, resulted in the concentration of practices in more affluent areas, undermining the availability of services in less affluent areas [10].

Access to and use of health care are necessary but not sufficient conditions for benefitting from health services. In the theoretical framework on access to services by Levesque et al., an important aspect of access is to have the possibility to use appropriate services or services which are evidence-based, effective, timely, and delivered efficiently to meet a patient's specific needs [11]. As suggested in Chap. 5, the appropriateness of care is dependent on how the services are organised and regulated and the mechanisms to secure adequate standards of services. However, if the services are not appropriate or there are differences between population groups in appropriateness of care, the full benefits of service in terms of health gains are compromised.

Ability to Engage in Health Care

As suggested in Fig. 6.2, factors related to an individual patient or the patient–professional relationship may also compromise the potential to benefit from health services. Patients' ability to engage in care and understand how and why the intervention is administered are important for the patients' adherence to the treatment regime and at the same time they are an indication of general health literacy [12]. On the providers' side, factors such as socioeconomic and ethnic biases, or lack of intercultural skills, may influence clinical decisions and lead to diagnostic delay or otherwise non-optimal treatment options [13, 14].

The ability to engage in health care relates according to Levesque et al. to 'the participation and involvement of the client in decision-making and treatment decisions… strongly determined by capacity and motivation to participate in care and commit to its completion' [4]. This dimension is related to individual (or family) resources, such as the capacity to communicate, as well as health literacy, self-efficacy, and self-management. While these resources are linked to the person's social position through factors like education, there is a risk that the challenges to patients' capability to participate in their care and comply with treatment regimens are not sufficiently taken into account in medical decision-making, care practices, and professional standards. Research has demonstrated that communication in health services is often qualitatively better and more successful with professionals and patients having similar social backgrounds [15]. However, it is possible to overcome these challenges and support the patients' ability to engage.

By going step by step through the process of gaining access to appropriate and effective health services and addressing both the supply (health system and service provision) and demand (population, patients) sides, the framework by Levesque et al. provides a tangible picture of how access to health care works and how the realisation of access and use of services is an interplay between the health system (as discussed in Chap. 5), health service providers and professionals, and patients from different population groups. The location of services, co-payments and other costs related to the use of services, and features of service provision reflecting professional values and practices are determined by the health system; a patient's chances to own a car to reach a provider, to have financial means to cover payments, and health capabilities and values to find services acceptable are socially and culturally determined. The clash of these features of service provision and the patients' abilities brings about social disparities in utilisation of services. However, we believe that by taking the limitations of accessibility among different socioeconomic and ethnic groups into account when designing health systems and services, it is possible to amend these disparities. The decisions required to do this are often aligned with societal values and political will and hence also related to structural determinants of health.

6.3 Differences in Treatment and Care

In addition to the accessibility of services, achieving the best possible health outcomes from health care use is associated with the content and quality of services. This is acknowledged by the framework by Levesque et al., which includes the appropriateness of health services and the patients' ability to access those appropriate services. While access to services may be conditioned by socioeconomic, geographical, cultural, and ethnic factors, these same factors can also influence the processes of service provision, such as the resources available and qualitative aspects of care, including continuity of care and the knowledge and interpersonal skills of the health care staff.

In several countries, health systems operate on socially differentiated tiers, e.g. for publicly insured and privately insured patients, impacting the actual resources and quality of services. Differences in the quality of care may affect non-medical aspects, such as hospitality of services, but often impact medical aspects as well. Apart from better access to services, the scope of services may be broader and the uptake of new treatments faster in health care providers serving higher socioeconomic groups with access to private insurance. While these factors are operating at the health system level addressed in Chap. 5, they also influence the medical decision-making latitude of healthcare professionals, patients' attitudes and trust towards healthcare providers, and interpersonal relationships between patients and professionals.

When addressing complicated treatments, the use of health services involves 'secondary access' and 'derived use', where the determining factor is a referral or recommendation by a doctor. In some health systems, this gatekeeping function for further care is stricter than in others. However, due to the asymmetry of medical knowledge and the agent–client relationship between health professionals and patients, the opinions of healthcare professionals are of primary importance for most healthcare use. Therefore, professionals' attitudes, clinical skills, understanding and knowledge of alternative treatment options and their effectiveness, as well as intercultural and interpersonal skills, and social and ethnic biases, impact variations in the use of health services among different population groups. In general, the use of specialist care shows more differences according to socioeconomic position than the use of primary care [16]. Research often shows that doctors' biased conceptions about poorer outcomes in disadvantaged groups and their lower engagement in care influence medical decisions regarding recommending demanding treatments to patients from these groups.

Like adding insult to injury, in efforts to incorporate social determinants of health into healthcare, there is a risk that social vulnerability may be transformed into a stigmatising risk factor. The research by Silva et al. [17] provides a comprehensive description of this phenomenon. It explains how, in the current healthcare environment, which relies heavily on extensive electronic recording of patient events, potentially erroneous perceptions of individual healthcare professionals can be propagated through electronic information systems (Box 6.1).

Box 6.1 Socioeconomic inequalities and health care documentation
In the study by Silva et al. [17], contradictions between electronic health records and patients' own narratives show that the practices of the health care system can unconsciously exacerbate existing socio-economic health inequalities. The key observations on the consequences of socio-economic differences in treatment and health care are:

- Translating social suffering into stigmatising risk factors: Patients' suffering due to socio-economic challenges, such as poverty, homelessness, or domestic violence, may be translated into individual, stigmatising risk factors in health professionals' documents. The individualisation can mask the structural causes behind health problems and lead to blaming patients or minimising their symptoms.

(*continued*)

6.3 Differences in Treatment and Care

Box 6.1 (continued)

- Questioning patients' trustworthiness based on socioeconomic factors: Physicians may use information about patients' socioeconomic backgrounds as evidence of their untrustworthiness as a patient. For example, patient records may refer to social risks when a patient does not follow treatment instructions or questions diagnoses, instead of seeing these reactions as a possible result of mistrust or negative experiences.
- Negative impacts of healthcare encounters: Negative interactions experienced by patients in health care related to their socioeconomic background can lead to feelings of shame, fear, and frustration. These feelings, in turn, can reduce patients' willingness to seek treatment or trust the healthcare system.
- Differences between patient experiences and doctor's labels: Patients' own experiences and views on the causes and treatment of their health problems often differ from doctors' labels, which may emphasise medical risk factors and neglect or interpret the socioeconomic context. This can lead to misunderstandings and a lack of trust between the patient and the healthcare professional.
- The impact of resistance and distrust on quality of care: When patients experience distrust or resistance to health care due to their socioeconomic background, it can manifest as reduced participation in care, questioning medical expertise, or opposition to treatment recommendations. This can reduce the quality of care they receive and lead to worse health outcomes.
- Making the role of the health care system invisible as a social determinant of health: Patient records often do not record how health care encounters themselves can be a social determinant of health that either mitigates or exacerbates health inequalities. Patients' negative experiences and their resulting resistance may be interpreted as their individual characteristics instead of recognising the role of the health care system itself in this.

The study highlights that reducing health inequalities is not just a technical challenge or asking the right questions to patients. It is important to understand how the documentation of socioeconomic risk factors can be stigmatising and influence the interpretations and treatment decisions of healthcare professionals. In addition, the health system's own actions can affect patients' trust and participation in care, which can further deepen socioeconomic health inequalities. The study suggests that involving patients in the creation of their own medical records could help reduce misunderstandings and build trust.

Similar to electronic information systems, the use of algorithms and artificial intelligence to support medical decision-making presents a new challenge for addressing inequalities in healthcare. Inequalities in access and outcomes are perpetuated when large databases, reflecting existing disparities in health care, are used to train decision-making algorithms and large language models. This can lead to biased medical decisions and further exacerbate health disparities. Therefore, it is crucial to ensure that these technologies are developed and implemented with careful consideration of existing inequalities. Efforts should be made to use diverse and representative data sets and to continuously monitor and adjust algorithms to prevent biased outcomes (Box 6.2).

> **Box 6.2 Algorithms and Differential Access to Care**
> Differential access to care can find ways of expression that are difficult to observe for patients, the wider public and even for health care professionals. It may be hidden in algorithms, used by health care providers. Prediction models, decision aids, and Artificial Intelligence (AI) applications contain algorithms that may reproduce or increase inequality in access to diagnosis or treatment and thus influence inequality. A recent review of studies evaluating demographic biases in large language models used for AI tools showed that over 90% of studies reported gender and ethnic biases [18]. Many prediction models contain ethnicity or race as a variable, at least in the USA [19]. They work through 'the data used to train algorithms often reflect[ing] structural inequities in health care systems arising from racism and its interactions with social determinants of health' [20]. A review shows that equity considerations are only seldom addressed [20]. Prediction models for the usefulness of screening for lung cancer, for example, take the life expectancy of patients into account and advise against screening with shorter life expectancy of patients. Life expectancy is group-based and contains ethnicity as a predictor of life expectancy. This variable improves the prediction models. However, it also reproduces inequality, because it represents the lack of access to life-saving care in the past [21].

Another dimension linked to inequalities in care is 'inequity by disease', first used by Jan De Maeseneer in a 'comment' in the *Lancet* on vertical disease programmes on non-communicable disease: '…. vertical programmes cause inequity for patients who do not have the "right" disease and create an internal brain-drain of health professionals' [22] (p. 1860). Vertical programmes are often used by international donors in low- and middle-income countries. In a 'perspectives article' in the Bulletin of WHO, De Maeseneer et al. pointed to the consequences of vertical, disease-oriented programmes: 'In many countries in the African continent, people living with HIV receive free care, food and educational grants for their children, whereas those with other diseases receive poor care and still have to pay out-of-pocket, leading to inequity by disease' [23] (p. 812). Although the concept of inequity by disease is associated with health care in low- and middle-income countries, equivalent cases can be found in high-income countries. In a personal communication, De Maeseneer pointed out that inequity by disease describes the situation 'where people with the same functional impact of a health condition, receive a different care package, against a different price, because they have different diagnosis.

An example: People with half-sided paralysis due to a brain tumour have different access to care packages and pay less than those with a half-sided paralysis after a brain haemorrhage. The reason is that in many EU countries separate 'Cancer programmes' exist, with a wider range of benefits'. An example from England concerns the difference between sickle cell patients and cancer patients. The drug hydroxyurea is free for cancer patients, but the costs for sickle cell patients are not fully covered by the NHS because this condition is not exempt from prescription charges unlike cancer. Patients with sickle cell disease pay a charge per prescription of 9.90 pounds (€ 11.88) or, with a prepayment certificate, 114.50 (€ 137.42) per year. People with sickle cell disease need long-term treatment. It is a hereditary disease that mainly affects people with African origin. Zainab Garba-Sani presented this example at the European Public Health Conference in 2024 in Lisbon. Inequity by disease also applies to broader disease categories. In many health systems, conditions, such as mental health disorders, are in fact deprioritised in terms of resources assigned to treating patients suffering from them. Despite research evidence on the effectiveness of treatment for mental health conditions compared to many somatic diseases, this deprioritisation is based on historical stigma of psychiatric conditions. As morbidities such as psychiatric conditions are more frequent among disadvantaged population groups, 'inequity by disease' in health care is a clear mechanism that reproduces social inequalities in health. Oral health suffers from similar differential treatment. Despite strong research evidence on poor oral health as a significant risk factor for multiple conditions and its impact on everyday functioning, oral health services are often separated from overall health systems and typically involve higher cost-sharing for patients.

6.4 Differential Benefits from the Use of Health Services and their Life Course Accrual

Above we referred to the definition of access by the Institute of Medicine which underlines that it is not only a question of having an option to use health services. It is also important to use services timely to achieve the best possible health outcomes [11]. We have seen that the interplay of people's (or their family's) resources and capabilities, on the one hand, and the health care system and professionals, on the other hand, may compromise the possibilities to use appropriate health services and to secure the best possible outcomes. In addition, there are several individual characteristics that may influence a person's ability to benefit from health care interventions. Many of these characteristics are related to social position and contribute to differentiated health outcomes, for example through the way patients respond to certain medications and treatments. Similarly, comorbidities or the presence of other health conditions can complicate treatment and affect outcomes. Mental health conditions, like depression and anxiety, can affect treatment adherence and recovery, making psychological support crucial for improving health outcomes. As referred earlier, patients' health literacy, or understanding of their health conditions and treatments, can influence their ability to follow medical advice and adhere to treatment plans. Habits such as diet, exercise, smoking, and alcohol consumption significantly impact treatment effectiveness. For example, a healthy lifestyle can improve recovery rates and overall health outcomes. Finally, individual preferences and values regarding treatment options can influence decision-making and satisfaction with care.

To take some of these individual variations into account is common medical practice in many health systems. Genetic variations are tested in order to choose effective treatment protocols in cancer therapy or the right medication in order to avoid adverse effects. Similarly, effectively managing comorbidities is customarily considered essential for optimising treatment benefits. However, also other individual factors, such as mental health, lack of health literacy, and an unhealthy lifestyle, can be considered as indicators of differentiated and often complex service needs that should be addressed within health services. There is growing understanding of individual and contextual factors that have an impact on the outcomes of care, but despite bold visions it is not well conceived how to take up a holistic approach that takes genetic, comorbid, socioeconomic, and cultural factors into account in developing optimal services to ensure the best possible health outcomes for all patients [24].

Another poorly understood area is the life course impact of health service on health disparities. Like inequalities in health [25], the disparities in outcomes of health services are often researched with a focus on individual services or treatments and usually in terms of short-term outcomes. Differential accumulated impacts of health services have not been studied, or the studies have used, for instance, complex indicators of a sentinel type, such as amenable mortality, in which the contributing factors are often difficult to disentangle, and which are thus difficult to operationalise [26, 27].

In Fig. 6.3, we give an overview of how the different kinds of health services are theoretically influencing health inequalities through their primary targets of impact in terms of health outcomes. Figure 6.3 is an adaptation from the publications by Diderichsen et al. [28–30] which review central mechanisms influencing socioeconomic differences in health and the policy entry points related to impacting health inequalities. We suggest that health services have similar entry points to health policies on their influence on social equality. In the original model, health care was considered as one of the policies. Here we underline the impact of health services and have added a box representing health care to the right side of the figure. Through this figure it is also possible to conceptualise the life-course cumulative effect of health services on inequalities in health.

In the original figure, Diderichsen and his co-workers demonstrated that different societal policies impact an individual's risks of becoming ill or being injured and consequences of illnesses and injuries by intervening on societal processes that determine the stratification of societies and people's potentials to end up in a certain social position, but also by decreasing health damaging exposures and vulnerability as well as specifically influencing consequences of ill health. In Fig. 6.3, we underscore that health care has just the same entry points to influence socioeconomic

6.4 Differential Benefits from the Use of Health Services and their Life Course Accrual 75

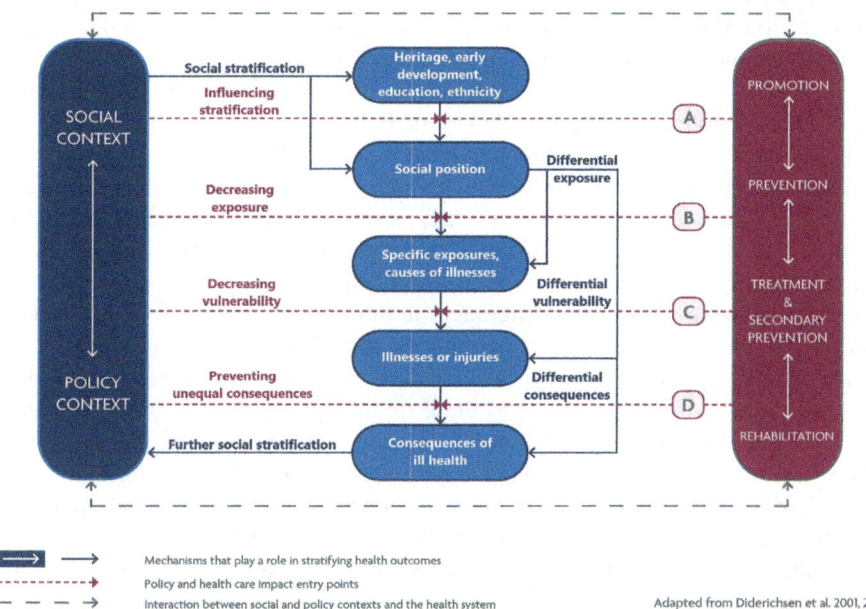

Fig. 6.3 Mechanisms influencing social equality in health and the policy and health care entry points related to impacting health inequalities; (A) Addressing discrepancies in health development, (B) Promoting healthy environments and preventing harmful exposures, (C) Decreasing susceptibility and vulnerability through interventions targeting high-risk individuals and populations, (D) Restoring health and preventing disparities in the consequences of illnesses and injuries. Source: authors' adaptation from [28, 29]

differences in health through the impacts of its different types of services which start with health promotion and prevention activities and end with care of chronic conditions, rehabilitation, and palliative care.

In early life, maternal services and well-baby clinics have been shown to be instrumental in supporting children's health and their performance in educational settings [31]. Depending on how these services are organised, they may either level social differences in children's and adolescents' health and educational achievements or, in case the access to or quality of these services favours the well-off, they may make these gradients steeper and enhance societal stratification. Similarly, it is important to consider how health services, such as occupational and environmental health care, addressing exposures related to work and housing, are influencing the levels of hazardous exposures and, in the end, people's differential risk to contract diseases or to get injured across socioeconomic groups.

In the case of health services treating individual persons, we have treatments which cure the disease and restore the person's health, but increasingly often we are speaking about chronic conditions where the treatment is meant to slow down the natural course of the disease and to postpone negative outcomes, or to keep the symptoms of the illness under control. With increasing survival and an ageing population, the challenge is to treat patients living with several chronic conditions and balance with different treatments to optimise the patient's functional capacity. In these cases, we are speaking about secondary or tertiary prevention and rehabilitation which do not cure but aim to prevent and postpone the onset of illness or to reduce the effects of an existing illness and to restore capabilities needed for daily life.

In the worst case, within an unequal health system, the effects of poor services accumulate and result in adverse health outcomes. These include high exposure to health risks, susceptibility to diseases, early onset of chronic morbidity and multimorbidity, reduced functional capacity, and premature death. Additionally, these factors contribute to and reinforce social stratification.

Emerging research on social differences in multimorbidity and chronic diseases over the life course suggests that such an accumulation of health risks leading to poor outcomes can be observed in several countries. However, research exploring the contribution of health services to these findings is scarce, if not non-existent. Similar to general morbidity and mortality, a clear gradient favouring the well-off in multimorbidity has been identified in many studies [32, 33]. Research also indicates that people living in more deprived areas have a higher risk of being diagnosed with chronic conditions and multimorbidity, and of dying at all ages [34].

In addition, cohort studies support the theory that sensitive age periods in early life are important in subsequent development of multimorbidity in later life and that a pathway of interconnected risk factors over the life course, where one adverse experience leads to another, results in an increased risk of multimorbidity [35]. While these findings are compatible with a potential impact of a range of social adversities, they also call for the need to study the contribution of poor health services to inequities in multimorbidity and to explore effective interventions for preventing increasing multimorbidity.

6.5 Conclusions

- The role of health services in creating and reproducing inequalities in health becomes visible in three steps: the use (or non-use) of health services, differences in treatment and care once people have gained access, and differences in the benefits of treatment or care and in the functional consequences of treatment or care.
- Gaining access to care is partly dependent on the organisation of service provision and partly on the socially patterned abilities and resources of people.
- The use of information systems and clinical algorithms may contain biased information, leading to differential treatment and quality of care.
- Many characteristics related to the social position of people may at the same time contribute to differential outcomes and consequences for people's daily functioning.
- Not much is known about the impact of health services on health disparities over the life course.

References

1. IKNL. Kanker in Nederland: sociaaleconomische verschillen. Deel I: verschillen vóór en rondom diagnose 2024 [Available from: https://iknl.nl/kanker-in-nederland-ses-rapport-1.
2. IKNL. Kanker in Nederland: sociaaleconomische verschillen. Deel II: verschillen rondom behandeling 2024 [Available from: https://iknl.nl/kanker-in-nederland-ses-rapport-2.
3. IKNL. Kanker in Nederland: sociaaleconomische verschillen. Deel III: Verschillen in overleving, verloop van kanker, kwaliteit van leven, werk en financiën en (na)zorg 2024 [Available from: https://iknl.nl/kanker-in-nederland-ses-rapport-3).
4. Levesque J-F, Harris MF, Russell G. Patient-centred access to health care: conceptualising access at the interface of health systems and populations. Int J Equity Health. 2013;12(18)
5. IOM. Committee on monitoring access to personal health care services. Washington DC: National Academies Press; 1993.
6. Muylle F, Van der Heyden J. Diabetes in België in kaart gebracht: resultaten BELHES 2018. Vlaams Tijdschrift voor Diabetologie. 2019;2:12–3.
7. Stormacq C, Van den Broucke S, Wosinski J. Does health literacy mediate the relationship between socioeconomic status and health disparities? Integrative review. Health Promot Int. 2019;34(5):e1–e17.
8. Rahman M, Rosenberg M, Flores G, Parsell N, Akter S, Alam A, et al. A systematic review and meta-analysis of unmet needs for healthcare and long-term care among older people. Heal Econ Rev. 2022;12:60.
9. Van Poel E, Collins C, Groenewegen PP, Spreeuwenberg P, Bojaj G, Gabrani J, et al. The Organization of Outreach Work for vulnerable patients in general practice during COVID-19: results from the cross-sectional PRICOV-19 study in 38 countries. Int J Environ Res Public Health. 2023;20:3165.
10. Isaksson D, Blomqvist P, Winblad U. Free establishment of primary health care providers: effects on geographical equity. BMC Health Serv Res. 2016;16:28.
11. IOM. Crossing the quality chasm: a new health system for the 21st century. Washington DC: Institute of Medicine; National Academies Press; 2001.
12. IOM. Health literacy: a prescription to end confusion. Washington DC: Institute of Medicine; National Academies Press; 2004.
13. Job C, Adenipekun B, Cleves A, Gill P, Samuriwo R. Health professionals implicit bias of patients with low socioeconomic status (SES) and its effects on clinical decision-making: a scoping review. BMJ Open. 2024;14:e081723.
14. Betancourt JR, Green AR, Carrillo JE, Ananeh-Firempong O II. Defining cultural competence: a practical framework for addressing racial/ethnic disparities in health and health care. Public Health Rep. 2003;118(4):293–302.
15. Verlinde E, De Laender N, De Maesschalck S, Deveugele M, Willems S. The social gradient in doctor-patient communication. Int J Equity Health. 2012;11:12.
16. Van Doorslaer EKA, Wagstaff A. Equity in the delivery of health care: some international comparisons. J Health Econ. 1992;11:389–411.
17. Silva JM, Durden TE, Hirsch A. Erasing inequality: examining discrepancies between electronic health records and patient narratives to uncover perceived stigma and dismissal in clinical encounters. Soc Sci Med. 2023;323:115837.
18. Omar M, Sorin V, Agbareia R, Apakama DU, Soroush A, Sakhuja A, et al. Evaluating and addressing demographic disparities in medical large language models: a systematic review. Int J Equity Health. 2025;24:57.
19. NASEM. Examining the history, consequences, and effects of race-based clinical algorithms on health equity: proceedings of a workshop. National Academies of sciences and medicine, editor. Washington, DC: The National Academies Press; 2023.
20. Cary MP Jr, Zink A, Wei S, Olson A, Yan M, Senior R, et al. Mitigating racial and ethnic bias and advancing health equity in clinical algorithms: a scoping review. Health Aff. 2023;42(10):1359–68.

21. Vaughan Sarrazin MS. Balancing statistical precision with societal goals to reduce health disparities using clinical support tools. JAMA Netw Open. 2023;6(9):e2331140.
22. De Maeseneer J, Roberts RG, Demarzo M, Heath I, Sewankambo N, Kidd MR, et al. Tackling NCDs: a different approach is needed. Lancet. 2012;379:1860–1.
23. De Maeseneer J, Li D, Palsdottir B, Mash B, Aarendonk D, Stavdal A, et al. Universal health coverage and primary health care: the 30 by 2030 campaign. Bull World Health Organ. 2020;98:812–4.
24. Fiandaca MS, Mapstone M, Connors E, Jacobson M, Monuki ES, Malik S, et al. Systems healthcare: a holistic paradigm for tomorrow. BMC Syst Biol. 2017;11:142.
25. Kivimäki M, Frank P. Tackling socioeconomic disparities in multimorbidity. Lancet Regional Health Europe. 2023;32:100689.
26. McCallum A, Manderbacka K, Arffman M, Leyland AH, Keskimäki I. Socioeconomic differences in mortality amenable to health care among Finnish adults 1992-2003: 12 year follow up using individual linked population register data. BMC Health Serv Res. 2013;13:3.
27. McMinn MA, Seaman S, Dundas R, Pell JP, Leyland AH. Socio-economic inequalities in rates of amenable mortality in Scotland: analyses of the fundamental causes using the Scottish longitudinal study, 1991–2010. Popul Space Place. 2020:e2385.
28. Diderichsen F, Evans T, Whitehead M. The social basis of disparities in health. In: Evans T, Whitehead M, Diderichsen F, Bhuiya A, Wirth M, editors. Challenging inequities in health From ethics to action. Oxford: Oxford University Press, 2001. p. 12–23.
29. Diderichsen F, Andersen I, Manuel C. Health inequality—determinants and policies. Scand J Public Health. 2012;40:12–105.
30. Diderichsen F, Hallqvist J, Whitehead M. Differential vulnerability and susceptibility: how to make use of recent development in our understanding of mediation and interaction to tackle health inequalities. Int J Epidemiol. 2019;48(1):268–74.
31. Melhuish E, Belsky J, Leyland AH, Barnes J. Effects of fully-established sure start local programmes on 3-year-old children and their families living in England: a quasi-experimental observational study. Lancet. 2008;372(9650):1641–7.
32. Álvarez-Gálvez J, Ortega-Martín E, Carretero-Bravo J, Pérez-Muñoz C, Suárez-Lledó V, Ramos-Fiol B. Social determinants of multimorbidity patterns: a systematic review. Front Public Health. 2023;11:1081518.
33. Pathirana TI, Jackson CA. Socioeconomic status and multimorbidity: a systematic review and meta-analysis. Aust N Z J Public Health. 2018;42(2):186–94.
34. Lyons J, Akbari A, Abrams KR, Lorenzo AA, Ba Dhafari T, Chess J, et al. Trajectories in chronic disease accrual and mortality across the lifespan in Wales, UK (2005–2019), by area deprivation profile: linked electronic health records cohort study on 965,905 individuals. Lancet regional health. Europe. 2023;32:1000687.
35. Wagner C, Carmeli C, Chiolero A, Cullati S. Life course socioeconomic conditions and multimorbidity in old age—a scoping review. Ageing Res Rev. 2022;78:101630.

Open Access This chapter is licensed under the terms of the Creative Commons Attribution 4.0 International License (http://creativecommons.org/licenses/by/4.0/), which permits use, sharing, adaptation, distribution and reproduction in any medium or format, as long as you give appropriate credit to the original author(s) and the source, provide a link to the Creative Commons license and indicate if changes were made.

The images or other third party material in this chapter are included in the chapter's Creative Commons license, unless indicated otherwise in a credit line to the material. If material is not included in the chapter's Creative Commons license and your intended use is not permitted by statutory regulation or exceeds the permitted use, you will need to obtain permission directly from the copyright holder.

Chapter 7
From Access to and Utilisation of Health Services to Equality in Population Health

7.1 Introduction

The question we address in this chapter is: How can we make the step from differential utilisation and benefits of health services to the consequences for population health equity? This is the right-hand upward pointing arrow in Fig. 2.1 in Chap. 2 (see Fig. 7.1).

Health systems are complex systems—non-linear systems involving multiple interdependent components and feedback loops [1]. As we saw, system complexity may in itself contribute to inequalities (see Chap. 4, Sect. 4.4). In Sect. 6.4, we have discussed the accumulation of health inequalities over the life course. The effects of health systems and service provision on differential utilisation and benefits are part of a dynamic system, with feedback loops, delayed effects, and interdependencies between actors in the system [2]. Systems science gives clues to approaches to the complexity of the transformation step. We explore a number of approaches without claiming to have a complete overview.

Socioeconomic inequalities in patient outcomes arise as a result of a gradient in access, utilisation, and benefits across socioeconomic groups, or through differential prevalence of patient groups across socioeconomic groups, or a combination of these. In an ideal situation, an individual using the health service will be restored to full health. For chronic conditions, although the incidence differs between social groups, health service utilisation should lead to equal levels of functional health. This means that the consequences of inequalities in the incidence of (non-fatal) disease would be eradicated by an efficient health service. Differential utilisation would then be the only source of inequality due to health care. However, the health service may introduce or increase health inequalities if there is a social gradient in benefits arising from health service utilisation, for example due to differences in case fatality following contact with the health service or in the extent of any recovery, as discussed in Chap. 6.

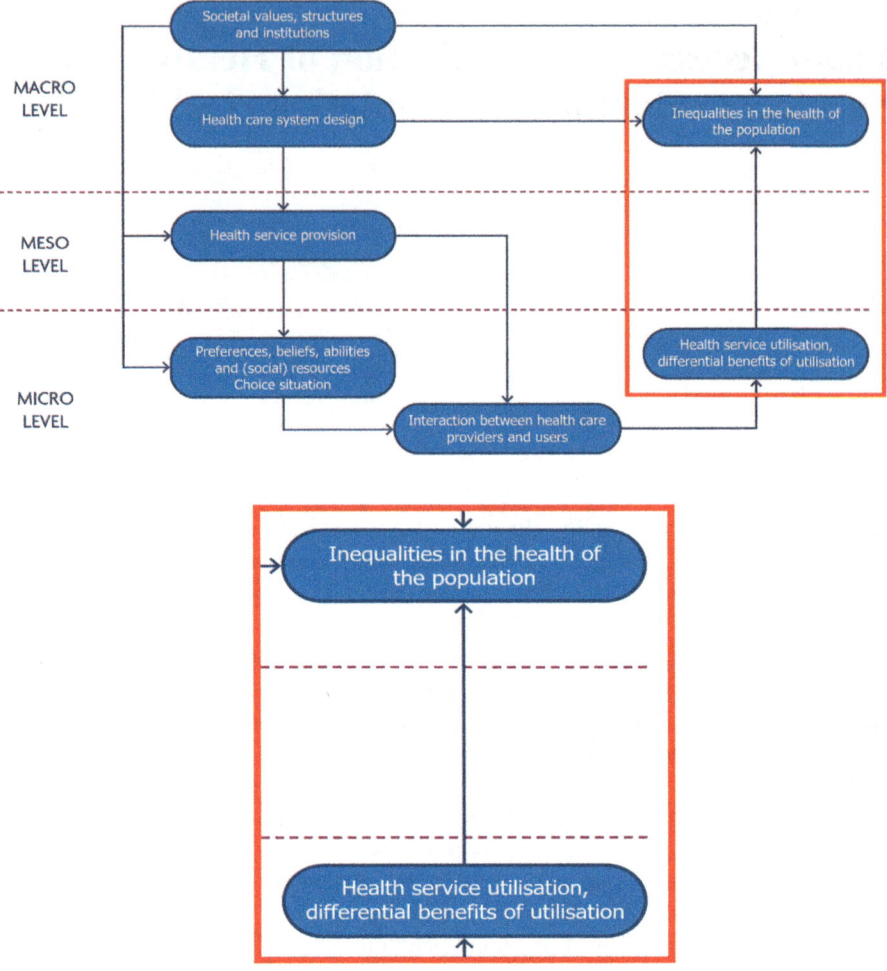

Fig. 7.1 Subsection of Fig. 2.1, highlighting the focus of this chapter

7.2 Why Simple Aggregation May Not Work, and Potential Solutions

A first and often neglected problem is: What is the population for which we want to assess effects of health service utilisation on population health equity? The definition of the population is central to social epidemiology. If we exclude undocumented people, homeless people, or people without public health insurance from the population, because information on their health care use is lacking, the extent of population health inequalities would be underestimated. Hence, the exact definition of what we see as the population is important.

If the definition of the population is clear and we have population-wide, individual-level information on needs for care and service use (and non-use) and the outcomes of service utilisation, and if this information is available by all relevant individual background characteristics, it would in theory be possible to transform this individual-level information to population-level inequality through aggregation. However, there are several problems encountered in the transformation from individual service utilisation and the benefits from service use to population health inequalities. Even with complete data available, the aggregation process would be very complicated and require a modelling approach.

Adding to the complexity is that outcomes in different sectors within the health care system, e.g. the mental health sector and primary care, can influence each other through side effects of treatment or possibly the accumulation of health problems as in comorbidities. Studies often deal only with a specific sector of health care or part of it, or a specific service or type of health problem. Hence, information is usually incomplete. There will be cumulative effects of inequalities along several different dimensions of inequality (see the discussion about intersectionality in Chap. 1). Another source of complexity is temporality. There will be time lags in the occurrence of health effects, feedback loops (that can be studied by analysing changes over time), and effects over people's life course. There are a number of solutions or at least partial solutions to the problem of transforming individual information to population level. The first two solutions that we will discuss in the following sections relate to the research design:

- Quasi-experiments and natural experiments
- Analysis of feedback loops and longitudinal analysis

The last three solutions relate to modelling approaches:

- Microsimulation and agent-based models
- Health impact analysis and
- Public health foresight studies

7.3 What Is the Population?

The definition of the population is not trivial. This may exclude certain groups, and these groups may be in worse health than the population that is included. This is the case when, for example, undocumented people or those in the process of seeking asylum are not included in the population. The fact that people are undocumented makes it difficult to include them in a population; the size and characteristics of this group are unknown. It may be that for some groups, such as homeless people, we can estimate their size; however, we also need information on their use or non-use of services and their health. This information may be hard to come by.

Population-based studies, such as surveys, that can be used to assess population health inequalities, are biased by the fact that some groups are under-represented because they are difficult to reach. Hard to reach populations are not a homogeneous category [3]. People may have reasons not to participate because of the mere fact that being known threatens their position, such as in undocumented people, or they may feel that their behaviours are stigmatised or illegal, such as people who use drugs. The reason of lack of participation may also be that the mode of administration of a survey requires a degree of literacy that people miss. This is exacerbated by reliance on digital data collection. Good knowledge of the difficult to reach populations and their involvement in studies by the researchers may attenuate the problem. The underlying reasons for not being reached or non-participation may relate to a background that also influence their health care seeking and access to care. This makes it difficult to use statistical approaches to solve under-representation. A standard approach such as weighting survey data to make the survey population representative of the target population is based on characteristics of individuals. However, if the pattern of health and health behaviour differs between the survey responders and non-responders, then the use of survey weights is not an option. An example from the Finnish health survey illustrates this. Despite a high response to the survey (85%), there was a different relationship between alcohol harms and mortality and education between survey responders and non-responders (information on both obtained through data linkage) [4]. Missing data lead to missing inequalities, as Alison McCallum, one of the discussants at a conference presentation of the outlines of this book, remarked. There are no simple recipes to solve this problem. Comparison of different sources, including registry data, and applying different methods, quantitative and qualitative, may be part of the solution.

The definition of the population may differ between health systems due to the use of a different terminology and be less relevant from a societal point of view. In health services research studies in the United States, population health often refers to the health of the population that is served by a certain health system and the term health system is used to describe hospitals and physicians that are affiliated with one organisation (see Chap. 1). In this case, there may be many populations, and they may form a selection to begin with and differ from the general population living in a geographical area.

7.4 Quasi-Experiments and Natural Experiments

Quasi-experimental or natural experimental designs are used to evaluate impacts of the exposure to an intervention in conditions that do not meet the requirements of a randomised controlled trial. Although the two are often used synonymously, in a quasi-experiment the researcher may have some influence over exposure allocation [5]. It is often difficult in practice to obtain clear evidence as to the impact of health service utilisation on population health and health inequalities, and even more so when looking at the impact of health systems. Evaluating the impact of a health care system is problematic because of the difficulty in identifying a control system which is as comparable as possible. The ideal control would be identical in all aspects apart from the intervention under investigation (the health care system); this will rarely be realistic. It may, however, be possible to evaluate a change in one country's health care system by making comparisons with countries exhibiting parallel trends in health prior to the intervention—the 'difference in differences' approach [6]. In the event of the identification of a single country as a control proving difficult, a synthetic control can be created through a weighted combination of several countries. This approach was used, for example, to evaluate England's teenage pregnancy strategy [7]. Federal countries with differences in the health care system and organisation between federal states provide an opportunity to compare within a general common framework of culture and regulation [8]. This makes comparison easier. A well-designed analysis of the introduction of cost-sharing in health care systems or in parts of a health care system and its differential effects on people with different characteristics relating to equality would be an example.

Health and health inequalities are not only influenced by health policy. The importance of the social determinants of health was emphasised in Chap. 2, and policy formation and implementation across numerous sectors (e.g. welfare, education, employment) have the potential to increase or decrease health inequalities. The use of natural or quasi-experimental methods for policy evaluation is standard in public health [9], but it is clear that many such studies evaluating the impact of a policy on health fail to consider the impact on health inequalities [10].

The analysis of the impact of health services or treatments is also difficult. Again, the problem lies in establishing the control condition. It would not be ethical to conduct a randomised trial for an existing service or treatment whose efficacy has been shown. For new treatments this is often possible, and we would then have evidence as to treatment effectiveness which, if results are provided by social group (or other axes of inequality), can form the basis of modelling or simulation studies to understand wider societal impacts. However, analysis by social group is often not provided in trials, because it is not seen as of high importance and hence not measured, or the study is inadequately powered to undertake the analysis. The alternative, relying on observational data to try to conduct quasi-experiments, will always be limited because it will not normally be possible to understand or replicate the rationale for clinical decision-making, which take into account detailed consideration of the patient's health and medical history, based on administrative data. Our recommendation is to power trials to be able to analyse the data across social groups.

7.5 Feedback Loops and Longitudinal Analysis

Outcomes of service utilisation and the experiences of patients may feedback to service providers and influence their future policies and decisions. Knowledge of unequal outcomes of treatment may lead to health care providers changing their approach or to patients avoiding these providers. This could be called first-order changes (see also Chap. 2, Sect. 2.4 and Fig. 2.3). Knowledge of unequal outcomes and patient experiences may also lead to changes in regulation and thus leading to changes in the health system (second-order changes). Performance information of health care organisations may lead to improvements through selection and change [11]. Selection occurs when performance information is used by patients to choose a service provider. This may displace service providers with bad performance. Improvement occurs when performance information feeds back to health care organisations and is used to change service provision. Equity in the practice population or service area could be part of performance information. These feedback loops are known as the learning health care system [12].

In Chap. 5, Sect. 5.4 about the acceptability of health services, we discussed the responsiveness of health service providers and health systems to patient expectations. Information about responsiveness may feedback from service users to service providers and decision-making authorities through formal channels, such as complaint procedures and informal channels, such as social media or healthcare provider review sites [13]. Catastrophic health spending, as a consequence of high user payments, may have a feedback loop to the health of people through the stress they experience. This effect on people's health may—later—impact on health service utilisation. This can be studied by longitudinal research designs.

7.6 Microsimulation and Agent-Based Models

Microsimulation models can be used to predict individual outcomes under specified conditions; through aggregation they are also able to predict population outcomes including studies of population health inequalities. These predictions are made based on knowledge of the (causal) relationships between variables obtained from different sources, either empirical or in the literature: randomised controlled trials, epidemiologic studies such as case–control and cohort studies, and meta-analyses [14]. Because microsimulation models can be used to replicate complex systems—subject to the availability of estimates of the different relationships—their strength is in the ability to vary the conditions that are specified. Such variations enable the modelling of long-term consequences (e.g. as the population ages) or the assessment of different policy scenarios through comparison with counterfactuals in ways that would not be possible through trials or observational studies. Examples of microsimulation studies of health inequalities in the literature include an investigation of the long-term economic consequences (in terms of healthcare costs) of socioeconomic inequalities in health [15] and a study projecting widening socioeconomic inequalities in the burden of multimorbidity over a 30-year period [16].

An alternative to microsimulation is agent-based modelling. Agent-based models (ABMs) again operate at the micro level but incorporate individual decision-making as a means of representing complex systems [17]. This agency of individuals is the key distinction between ABMs and microsimulation models since it enables the inclusion of feedback loops and spillover effects, with the behaviour of one individual potentially interacting with or impacting on the behaviour of others [18]. However, the additional complexity of ABMs clearly comes at a cost, with an increased number of assumptions required compared to microsimulation models.

7.7 Health Impact Analysis

Health impact studies aim to analyse and predict the impact on people's health of (proposed) policies in, or more usually, outside the health field. The best-known studies are those in the field of environmental impact. These analyse the impact of policy measures that affect the living environment on the health of the population, including the location of industrial plants or the construction of new roads. Increasingly, health impact studies also take the impact on health equity into account [19]. Such studies often combine quantitative models and qualitative analysis but may also involve rapid reviews of the evidence or stakeholder workshops.

Health impact analysis can also be used to analyse and predict the impact of changes in health policy, health services, and medical treatment [20]. For example, following treatment in the health service, patients may remain at increased risk of subsequent morbidity or mortality. The IMPACT model is a microsimulation model that has been developed to explore the contribution of changes to medical treatment and risk factors to coronary heart disease (CHD) mortality [21]. As such, the model assigns different risks to a number of mutually exclusive patient groups such as the kind of myocardial infarction, secondary prevention after revascularisation, and a primary pharmacological prevention group receiving statins [22].

7.8 Public Health Foresight Studies

Foresight studies aim to provide the tools to gain a better understanding of future developments in order to make better policy decisions [23]. Although foresight studies traditionally focused on (new) health technologies, this approach is also used to analyse broader trends and alternative scenarios. The tools used in public health foresight studies include scenario analysis, modelling studies (e.g. to estimate the trends in certain outcomes when known influences on these outcomes do not change), expert opinion, and stakeholder consultations. The basis for public health foresight studies is a conceptual model that describes the relationships between context, policies, actors, mechanisms, and outcomes. Due to the uncertainties in future developments, alternative scenarios are often used [24].

In the Netherlands, a special public health foresight report has been published to estimate the effects of the COVID-19 pandemic on population health [25]. Although not presented as such, this could be seen as a 'model' for the transformation of individual-level outcomes to population level. At each step in the care-pathway from testing for COVID-19 infection to—in the end—mortality, 'socioeconomic disparities became more pronounced' [26]. Moreover, during the pandemic non-COVID-related care was postponed; how this has affected inequalities in the long run is a step more complex due to time-effects [27].

For our challenge—transforming individual health care utilisation and benefits to the population level—a scenario estimating the trend in health inequalities, based on a broad range of health care sectors, would be most helpful. Equality is an important consideration in public health foresight studies, e.g. in the Dutch foresight studies that have been produced every 4 years since 1993. They provide trend information on education related differences in subjective health and lifestyle. The trend in subjective health is that the differences between people with high and low education increase during the considered foresight period (up till 2040) [28].

7.9 Conclusions

- The step from differential utilisation of and benefits from health services to population health inequalities is not realised by simple aggregation.
- An important step is a definition of the population we want to describe.
- Systems science gives clues to approaches to the complexity of the transformation step; foresight studies, health impact analysis, microsimulation, and agent-based models may provide tools for this.
- We have to take into account mutual influences between sectors in the health system, feedback effects, and cumulative effects along dimensions of inequality and over the life course.
- We have discussed a number of approaches that may be helpful in the transformation of individual outcomes in terms of differential utilisation of and benefits from health services to population health inequalities. However, this remains the biggest challenge in the whole system approach we have discussed throughout our book.

References

1. Rutter H, Savona N, Glonti K, Bibby J, Cummins S, Finegood DT, et al. The need for a complex systems model of evidence for public health. Lancet. 2017;390:2602–4.
2. Diez Roux AV. Complex systems thinking and current impasses in health disparities research. Am J Public Health. 2011;101:1627–34.
3. Shaghaghi A, Bhopal RS, Sheikh A. Approaches to recruiting 'hard-to-reach' populations into research: a review of the literature. Health Promotion Perspectives. 2011;1(2):86–94.
4. McMinn MA, Gray L, Härkänen T, Tolonen H, Pitkänen J, Molaodi OR, et al. Alcohol-related outcomes and all-cause mortality in the health 2000 survey by participation status and compared with the Finnish population. Epidemiology. 2020;31(4):534–41.
5. de Vocht F, Katikireddi SV, McQuire C, Tilling K, Hickman M, Craig P. Conceptualising natural and quasi experiments in public health. BMC Med Res Methodol. 2021;21:32.
6. Craig P, Katikireddi SV, Leyland A, Popham F. Natural experiments: an overview of methods, approaches, and contributions to public health intervention research. Annu Rev Public Health. 2017;38:39–56.
7. Baxter AJ, Dundas R, Popham F, Craig P. How effective was England's teenage pregnancy strategy? A comparative analysis of high-income countries. Soc Sci Med. 2021;270:113685.
8. Bennema-Broos M, Groenewegen PP, Westert GP. Social democratic government and spatial distribution of health care facilities: the case of hospital beds in Germany. Eur J Pub Health. 2001;11:160–5.

9. Craig P. Natural and quasi-experiments. In: Detels R, Abdool Karim Q, Baum F, Li L, Leyland AH, editors. Oxford textbook of global public health. Seventh edition ed. Oxford: Oxford University Press; 2021.
10. Sell K, Rabbani S, Burns J. How is health equity considered in policy evaluations employing quasi-experimental methods? A scoping review and content analysis. Eur J Pub Health. 2025;35:42–51.
11. Berwick DM, James B, Coye MJ. Connections between quality measurement and improvement. Med Care. 2003;41:I-1-I-8.
12. Grossmann C, Powers B, McGinnis JM. Digital infrastructure for the learning health system: the Foundation for Continuous Improvement in health and health care. Institute of Medicine. Washington DC: National Academies Press; 2011.
13. Khan G, Kagwanja N, Whyle E, Gilson L, Molyneux S, Schaay N, et al. Health system responsiveness: a systematic evidence mapping review of the global literature. Int J Equity Health. 2021;20:112.
14. Rutter CM, Zaslavsky AM, Feuer EJ. Dynamic microsimulation models for health outcomes: a review. Med Decis Mak. 2011;31:10–8.
15. Horvath T, Leoni T, Reschenhofer P, Spielauer M. Socio-economic inequality and healthcare costs over the life course - a dynamic microsimulation approach. Public Health. 2023;219:124–30.
16. Head A, Birkett M, Fleming K, Kypridemos C, O'Flaherty M. Socioeconomic inequalities in accumulation of multimorbidity in England from 2019 to 2049: a microsimulation projection study. Lancet Public Health. 2024;9:e231–e9.
17. Silverman E, Gostoli U, Picascia S, Almagor J, McCann M, Shaw R, et al. Situating agent-based modelling in population health research. Emerg Themes Epidemiol. 2021;18:10.
18. Arnold KF, Harrison WJ, Heppenstall AJ, Gilthorpe MS. DAG-informed regression modelling, agent-based modelling and microsimulation modelling: a critical comparison of methods for causal inference. Int J Epidemiol. 2019;48:243–53.
19. Buse CG, Lai V, Cornish K, Parkes MW. Towards environmental health equity in health impact assessment: innovations and opportunities. Int J Public Health. 2019;64:15–26.
20. Wanjohi NW, Harrison R, Harris-Roxas B. Health impact assessments of health sector proposals: an audit and narrative synthesis. Int J Environ Res Public Health. 2021;18:11466.
21. Unal B, Critchley JA, Capewell S. IMPACT, a validated, comprehensive coronary heart disease model. Liverpool: University of Liverpool; 2007.
22. Hotchkiss J, Davies CA, Dundas R, Hawkins N, Jhund PS, Scholes S, et al. Explaining trends in Scottish coronary heart disease mortality between 2000 and 2010 using IMPACTSEC model: retrospective analysis using routine data. Br Med J. 2014;348:g1088.
23. Lapão LV, Peyroteo M, Dimnjakovic J, Gyimesi M. Overview of current foresight activities in Europe and beyond 2024 [Available from: https://www.phiri.eu/sites/default/files/2021-10/D9.1_Foresight%20Final%20Report_0.pdf.
24. Verschuuren M, Hilderink HBM, Vonk RAA. The Dutch public health foresight study 2018: an example of a comprehensive foresight excercise. Eur J Pub Health. 2019;30(1):30–5.
25. RIVM. Corona-inclusieve VTV 2020 [Available from: https://www.volksgezondheidtoekomstverkenning.nl/c-vtv.
26. Meulman I, Uiters E, Cloin M, Struijs J, Polder JS, Stadhouders N. From test to rest: evaluating socioeconomic differences along the COVID-19 pathway in The Netherlands. Eur J Health Econ. 2024;25(9):1581–1594.
27. Frey A, Tilstra AM, Verhagen MD. Inequalities in healthcare use during the COVID-19 pandemic. Nat Commun. 2024;15(1):1894.
28. RIVM. Gezondheidsverschillen: Hoe ontwikkelen zich gezondheidsverschillen in de toekomst? 2018 [Available from: https://www.vtv2018.nl/gezondheidsverschillen.

Open Access This chapter is licensed under the terms of the Creative Commons Attribution 4.0 International License (http://creativecommons.org/licenses/by/4.0/), which permits use, sharing, adaptation, distribution and reproduction in any medium or format, as long as you give appropriate credit to the original author(s) and the source, provide a link to the Creative Commons license and indicate if changes were made.

The images or other third party material in this chapter are included in the chapter's Creative Commons license, unless indicated otherwise in a credit line to the material. If material is not included in the chapter's Creative Commons license and your intended use is not permitted by statutory regulation or exceeds the permitted use, you will need to obtain permission directly from the copyright holder.

Chapter 8
The Added Value of Integrating the Three Areas and the Way Forward

8.1 The Substantive Question and the Intermediate Steps

The answer to the question whether the design of health care systems and inequalities in population health are related is positive. The design of health systems is related to population health inequalities. According to an analysis of the World Health Organisation Regional Office for Europe, 10% of the inequalities in self-reported health and 11% of the inequalities in mental health are attributable to health services, including the organisation and funding of the system. Over time, the influence of health care on population health has increased. The design of health systems and health care provision has affected health inequalities. What is it in the design of health care systems that coincides with more inequality in population health? The way of funding health care and in particular out-of-pocket payments, and the complexity of health systems and of the organisation of health insurance, create inequalities. The introduction of market elements and cost-sharing has most probably increased inequality. A strong primary care system is related to less inequality in access and perhaps also in health outcomes. For inequalities in access this is clear, but the evidence-base for inequalities in health outcomes is still weak. Involvement of the population (community engagement) in health care has the potential to improve inequalities in health. Addressing health inequalities requires community advocacy and co-design at different levels.

The underlying explanation for the relationship between the design of health systems and population health equity is that both are influenced by the structure of society. Health care systems reflect society's values, economy, and politics, and so does population health equity. Welfare and health care system ideologies vary from people caring for themselves in market-oriented systems, people caring for each other in insurance systems, and the state caring for people in national health and welfare systems. National health systems consider access to health care as every citizen's right and value equity for everybody. Social Health Insurance systems

© The Author(s) 2026
P. P. Groenewegen et al., *Health Systems, Health Services and Inequality in Population Health*, SpringerBriefs in Public Health,
https://doi.org/10.1007/978-3-032-02565-4_8

focus on the right of those insured with a potential exclusion of those who are—for whatever reasons—not insured. Private health care systems rely on market elements, and private insurance and payments. Government participation according to the agendas of left-wing political parties is related to the development of strong primary care and to more equitable health care systems. Currently, populist right-wing political parties are beginning to participate in the government of a number of European countries. How they will affect health care and inequality in population health has not yet been empirically assessed but is a research priority for the future.

The pathway from the design of health systems to inequalities in population health runs via service provision and service utilisation. The design of health systems influences important aspects of service provision. From the point of view of inequalities in service provision, accessibility of care is central. Accessibility is multidimensional and affects different population groups in different ways. It is related to the design of health systems, but this link has seldom been studied in international, comparative research. Health systems where health care providers are respnisible for a defined population and which provide strong primary care are beneficial for several aspects of accessibility. The availability of care providers is a growing problem in health care, exacerbated by demographic changes in society, the demands of health care work, and the balance with private life. Availability is a big problem in remote rural areas, but in private health systems it is also problematic in inner city areas, leading to inequalities in accessibility. The affordability of care benefits from universal health coverage in terms of population, services, and costs covered. Accessibility differs across social groups; for example, there are inequalities in receipt of appropriate care by ethnic groups as a result of implicit or explicit discrimination and exclusion, but there is a lack of research into these phenomena outside the United States.

Just as accessibility is multidimensional, so is actual access and the use of services. However, it is not only the use or non-use of services that may influence inequalities. The quality of treatment and care and the responsiveness or person-centredness of the provided services differ for patients with different socioeconomic backgrounds. And even with equal access and equal treatment/care, some patients may benefit more from the treatment/care they receive, depending on their capabilities and circumstances. This leads to different functional consequences in the long run, although not much is known about the impact of health services on health disparities over the life course.

The final step in the pathway from differential service use and benefits to inequalities in population health is still a big challenge in a whole-system approach, but we were able to suggest a number of elements to move from service use—or non-use for that matter—by individual patients to see the impact at the population level. Simple aggregation does not do the trick (in most cases). However, a first issue to solve is the definition of the population. If the definition of the population excludes certain groups that have a low socioeconomic status or who are otherwise vulnerable and have worse health, population health inequalities will be underestimated. The population definition should be inclusive, and researchers should be more aware of the social and health status of difficult to reach groups. The step from differential utilisation of and benefits from health services to population health equity is not realised by simple aggregation. Systems science gives clues to approaches to the complexity of the transformation from individual outcomes to the macro level of inequalities in population health. Public health foresight studies, health impact analysis, microsimulation, and agent-based models may provide tools to undertake this transformation step.

8.2 The Added Value of Combining Health Systems, Health Services, and Population Health Research

This book shows that there is added value in combining the three areas of research. It is not easy to separate the research added value from the policy added value. Research in the three areas is not done in a policy vacuum. The questions we pose and the issues we study are based on the problems that policymakers and practitioners encounter in the health care sector of society. These problems are being transformed into research problems (see Fig. 8.1). In the empirical cycle of research within a specific discipline, the problems for research are generated within that discipline, and usually based on previous research. However, health systems, health services, and population health research are part of a broader cycle that also involves application of the results in health policy.

Also, the research designs are often influenced by what is a suitable and feasible design for studies that use data from health service users and providers. The relationship between the health sector and research also implies that a transformation is required from the research results as such back to the problems of policymakers in the sector, with implementation often running via intermediary groups, such as local

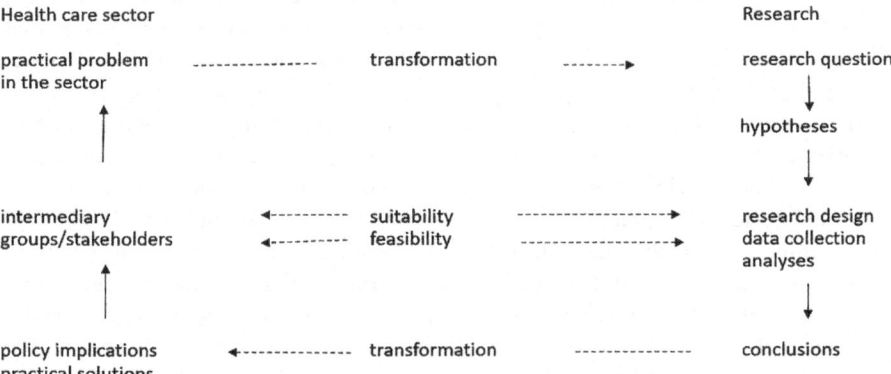

Fig. 8.1 Relationships between sector of health care and health system, health services and population health research. Source: Reproduced from Leyland & Groenewegen 2020 [1], Figure 1.3. A minor modification was made. https://doi.org/10.1007/978-3-030-34801-4_1, licensed under the terms of the Creative Commons Attribution 4.0 International License (http://creativecommons.org/licenses/by/4.0/)

health authorities, insurance organisations, or hospitals. It may be argued that there is a risk when the connections between research and policy are very close. However, researchers do not have to develop policy themselves; they should make the results of their research relevant and useful to policy.

As we have shown in the previous chapters, the design of health systems, which is influenced by the structure and institutions of societies, influences health service provision, utilisation and its benefits for people, with effects on population health inequalities. However, usually these research areas, and thus parts of the diagram in Fig. 2.1 in Chap. 2, are studied in isolation. Studies that address the overlapping area between health systems, health services, and population health research are very rare. In particular, the impact of differential health service utilisation on inequalities in population health has been neglected. Not only is research divided along these lines, health policy making at national and intermediate levels is also often fragmented with, for example, separate departments within ministries of health. This affects the 'demand' for integrated studies (see Sect. 8.5).

Health system design and service provision impact on inequalities in population health in both positive and negative manners. This invites us to ask new questions, such as: How do changes in health system design affect inequalities in population health? Health service provision not only affects inequalities in service utilisation but also generates or diminishes inequalities in treatment quality and benefits. Access to high-quality health care is a key determinant of inequalities. The reduction of population health inequalities thus requires more than population-level interventions in the social determinants of health, although these are of unquestionable importance. Usually, treatments are only evaluated in terms of their impact on patients and not based on their population-level impact. Combining the three areas of research requires a broader definition of outcomes in health services research: not only outcomes for individual patients but also the consequences for inequalities at the population level.

The step from differential service utilisation and benefits to inequalities in population health is not a simple one. We have suggested a number of approaches that may be helpful in making this step. Some of these approaches are more qualitative, such as health impact analysis and public health foresight studies that use stakeholder information and expert opinion, others more quantitative, such as microsimulation models. In this book, we have given a partial answer to the question: How can health service utilisation be transformed to the population level?

Health system design and service provision have a limited but certainly not negligible impact on health inequalities at a population level, as shown in Chap. 4. Moreover, over time, the influence of health care on population health has increased, particularly in high income countries. Inequalities in society, the design of health systems, and service provision have common backgrounds in values of the population, political views, and the structure and institutions of society. Through this common background, health systems and service provision may have a bigger impact on population-level health inequalities than the estimated 10–11% cited in Chap. 4. This means that interventions at the health care system and service provision levels to tackle inequalities in health are important. Lack of development and implementation of such interventions designates an implicit priority of maintaining the current organisation of health systems and services.

Some of the required changes in health systems to improve population health and equality are well-known: universal health coverage, lower out-of-pocket costs and improved accessibility (along all dimensions). Changes come at a cost and the benefits often only materialise in the future and arise in areas other than the health care budget. However, inequalities in population health also come with costs that are difficult to assess. The population health inequality impacts of health system changes are important but are seldom analysed. Health systems (as all social systems) tend to resist changes (although health system changes are easier in some countries, depending on the political system), and vested interests are strong. Patients and citizens have the weakest position in this. Nevertheless, health systems may be easier to change than the societal structures underlying inequalities (the structural determinants of health).

The responsibility of the health care system and services for social determinants of health inequalities is gradually increasing and this is a result of policies and not of autonomous changes. Patient-reported outcomes are used alongside clinical outcomes and the former are not only determined by health service provision but also by social circumstances. In some sectors of health care, notably in primary care, a population orientation and outreach approach become more important. There is increasing awareness of the role of prevention in health service provision, apart from vaccination and screening programmes. To prevent the onset and worsening of chronic diseases, lifestyle programmes have been developed. Implementation of these programmes is more difficult for people who need them most and they can only be implemented when social circumstances and the role of social networks are taken into account. However, there is also a general societal trend of individualisation and in combination with pro-market policy approaches this leads to deliberate shifts of responsibility to individuals with a risk of increasing inequalities rather than diminishing them.

In an interview with *Medisch Contact* (the weekly of the Royal Dutch Medical Association, KNMG), prof. Jan Kremer noted that over time views on appropriate care have changed. In the past century, the view of professionals was from a position of leadership, for example in the development of guidelines in the last decades of the previous century. During the first decade of twenty-first century, the view of patients and their preferences were included in what was seen as appropriate care. Patients have a place in guideline development and there is increasing attention to shared decision-making. Finally, a shift towards the inclusion of a societal viewpoint in what is seen as appropriate care has occurred [2]. In the last few years, this has increasingly been seen, when weighing the costs of expensive (cancer) treatments against societal benefits, not only in economic terms, but also in terms of population wellbeing and inequality. Where outcomes are concerned this is, to put it simply, a move from morbidity and mortality (as health care provider-oriented outcomes) to quality adjusted life years (as patient-oriented outcomes) to population health and wellbeing and to population health inequality (as society-oriented outcomes). In a sense this development also reflects the three areas of research that we brought together in this book. Health systems are largely (still) built around professionals and managers of health care, with different incentives and interests and little influence of patients and the population (apart from elections). Health services research brings in the interaction between service providers and service users, the patients, while population health research brings in the effects at the macro level of society.

The latter development towards inclusion of the population-level benefits of (new) treatments provides a good argument for integrating health systems, health services, and population health research. Changes or interventions in health systems, health service provision, and the use of treatments and rehabilitation services must also be evaluated on the basis of their contribution to population health and inequalities in population health.

An equitable health care system and service provision is a necessary condition for equity in health but not enough; the social and economic consequences of ill health also have to be addressed, e.g. by a system of protection against income loss.

8.3 Elements of a Research Agenda

Research agendas are aligned with contexts and depend on national or regional needs. It is therefore difficult to sketch the outlines of a research agenda that could be universally applied. Nevertheless, we are keen to highlight a number of issues that could inform a research agenda.

Whole-System Approach

The previous chapters have shown that a whole-system approach will benefit the study of health inequalities. In comparing health systems, we have to be aware of differences in definitions of (health care) equality between countries or cultures. In many countries, the equity objectives are based on a fixed minimum service package, while in others the service package is much broader. Also, some parts of the population may be excluded from receiving the services. The approach towards equality may differ for health services and health outcomes. Equal access to health services provides equality of opportunity and not necessarily equality of outcomes. How these differences between countries can be explained and how they influence inequalities in the health of the population are important challenges for research.

Inequalities in society, the design of health care systems, and service provision have common backgrounds in population values and in political views and decisions. This is an area that needs more research. Related to this is a definition of the boundaries between health care systems, health systems, and welfare systems, and of the population. Changes in health service provision towards taking social determinants of health into account and policies and interventions to stimulate this deserve attention. What is the societal background of these policies? Are they effective and do they contribute to a reduction of health inequalities at the population level?

The impact of the participation of populist right-wing political parties in governments, and the policies they introduce or change, is an area in need of more research. A detailed analysis of who is excluded from receiving health and welfare benefits and on what grounds in the policies of countries with such parties in government is an important step. The ascent of populist right-wing political parties in Europe also influences the position of other parties when the former are not part of government. This may form a part of the explanation of the decreased strength of the relationship between government participation of left-wing political parties and inequality.

Research Designs and Methodology

Our whole-system approach of combining health systems, health services, and population health research has implications for research designs and methodology. Where experimental research is often impossible, quasi-experimental studies are important. For example, research into and modelling of the health inequality impacts of health system changes could be further developed. In comparative health systems research, a multilevel framework is important, ideally with a sufficient number of countries/health systems at the highest level. Multilevel analysis makes it possible to analyse health systems (and broader country characteristics), health service provision, and patient outcomes in a single analysis [1]. However, the step from patient outcomes to the population level cannot be made in a multilevel analysis.

Figure 2.1 does not contain the confounding variables that we would need to include in a statistical analysis. Confounding plays a role at all levels. Health systems influence service provision through their design, but provision is also influenced by characteristics that are only indirectly related to health system design, such as the economy or demographic characteristics.

The research agenda should acknowledge both qualitative and quantitative research. Qualitative research can, for example, lay the foundations for defining and operationalising intersectionality, in a move from single axes of inequality (income, education, etc.) to addressing the cumulative and interacting effects of combinations of dimensions. Qualitative policy analysis is also important in understanding the relationships between societal structures and institutions that form the structural determinants of health and the design of health systems.

Transformation of Inequalities in Population Health

The transformation of health service utilisation and differential benefits to inequalities in health at the population level are core problems that need more research. Figure 2.1 in Chap. 2 illustrates the pathways but is static. It does not include changes over time in health care systems or service provision or feedback loops from inequalities in the health of the population to health care system design or service provision. An increase in the supply of services may diminish shortages and reduce inequalities in health; however, this only happens under the condition that increased supply diminishes previously unmet needs of parts of the population and does not increase (over-)utilisation of services among other parts of the population.

There is a lack of knowledge about the accumulation of the impact of health services on health inequality over the life course and about delayed effects. Changes in utilisation patterns probably do not have immediate effects at the population level but only appear after some time. This makes the transformation from health service utilisation to its benefits at a population level more difficult.

Specific Health Care Sectors

From a population health inequality point of view, several sectors of health systems may deserve more attention. The first sector is primary care with an important impact on accessibility; however, effects on population health inequality are often hypothesised or assumed but seldom studied empirically. In Sect. 4.6, we discussed a number of characteristics of primary care that would facilitate policies to increase equality. They emphasise person- and population-centred care organisation that is currently an important policy area. Evaluations of these policy initiatives should include the effects on equality of access, treatment, and outcomes.

The second sector we may highlight is dental care. Dental care may be a relatively simple area in which to study the complete Fig. 2.1. Moreover, dental care is marginalised in most health systems, shows large inequalities, and there is increasing evidence of the broader effects of bad oral health on other diseases. Dental care also shows that within one country different health system designs exist, with different values and political acceptance. The United Kingdom's National Health Service, for example, is based on universal coverage and access; however, dental care is organised differently and much more open to the private sector and co-payments than is the case for the rest of health care.

Mental health care is another example of a sector that is often left out of comparative health systems research. The prevalence of mental health problems is increasing, particularly among young people, with potential long-term effects on population health inequality. There are large differences between socioeconomic groups in prevalence of mental health problems and access to services is problematic in most health care systems.

8.4 Conditions for Integration and Collaboration

Throughout this book and in particular in the previous two sections, we have shown the added value of integrating health systems, health services, and population health research. We have outlined the elements of a research agenda, but to develop this agenda further and to undertake the actual research contained in it requires integration and collaboration.

The three areas of research discussed in this book tend to work on their own. Although seen from a distance, the three approaches seem very close—some would say they are all part of public health research in a broad sense—but the researchers working in health systems, health services, and population health research come from different disciplines with different research cultures. Researchers of health systems often have a social science background in political science and policy studies. Health services researchers have a broad range of disciplinary backgrounds, ranging from social sciences and economics to clinical disciplines. And population health researchers often have a background in social epidemiology, demography, and statistics. Closer collaboration between health systems, health services, and population health researchers has added value for research and policy. In our view, it is therefore useful to see how we could break down the silos in which they operate.

The question in this last section of our book is therefore: How do we break down the silos? We will discuss a number of potential solutions and questions. We see potential solutions in four areas: the organisation of research, publication venues and conferences, capacity building and career opportunities, and finally funding of research. Preceding these potential solutions and in line with Fig. 8.1, we should be aware that not only research is divided along the lines of health systems, health services, and population health, but also health policy making at national and intermediate levels is often fragmented. Politicians and policymakers should be persuaded that in the end policy making aims at improving the level and distribution of population health. This conviction should ideally lead to a demand for integrated studies.

First Solution: The Practical Organisation of Research

From the bottom up, researchers may seek collaboration; however, this should be stimulated from the top down by their organisations (research institutes, universities, etc.). Research organisations could try to make teams of researchers that cover the three approaches. This would increase the opportunities to learn from the different approaches and work together in multidisciplinary teams. Apart from diversity in approaches, research teams, in particular when studying inequalities in health and care, could also benefit from diversity in sociodemographic background of researchers [3] and from participation of the people being studied [4].

Barriers to collaboration are that separate research organisations and academic departments have their main focus on either health systems or health services research or population health research. When research organisations or university departments focus on more than one area, for example primary care and population health/public health and epidemiology—which we see in the Netherlands and Belgium—the internal organisation is often in separate groups. Barriers are bigger when there is competition between the organisations that focus on each of the research areas.

It should be noted that silos and specialisation may also have advantages; some researchers are only or mainly interested in a certain subject or aspect and study this in depth. This raises the question which parts of research have to be done in collaboration and which can be done separately? And related to this question: Should we focus on multidisciplinary teams for primary empirical research or rather for synthesis of existing research?

Second Solution: Publication Venues and Conferences

High impact journals—important in the academic incentive structure—reinforce specialisation. There is a need for high impact journals that publish research that integrates the three fields. To do so, journals must broaden beyond clinical and disease-specific research. At the same time, high impact factors of journals only measure one aspect of impact. Referring to Fig. 8.1, impact on the health system and on society is also important. Broader societal impact is often not at the level of individual research projects, but of programmes of research. This is perhaps one of the reasons why journals are not yet so interested in societal impact. Although there is by now a long tradition of measuring (or attempts to measure) the impact of research, beyond the academic impact, the change in the academic reward system is much slower [5, 6].

Societal impact is not measured by the numbers of citations in academic journals. It may require a more narrative approach, for example based on interviews with decision-makers and analysis of policy documents. Impacts may be seen on actual care processes, on policy, and ultimately on population health, with increasing difficulties in attribution.

As with journals, conferences also tend to be specialised. They would be the ideal meeting places for researchers that work in different areas, provided that they include researchers with an interest in health systems, health services, and population health. Conferences should be motivated to organise multidisciplinary workshops that focus on different causes of population health equity (environment, social structures, power structures, intersectionality, health systems, and health service provision). Meeting each other and working together may help to overcome the barrier of different languages and variation in terminology between disciplines.

Third Solution: Capacity Building and Career Opportunities

First of all, we think that researchers need more than methods and statistics courses. They need to become acquainted with theories and methods from other disciplines to be able to work productively in multidisciplinary settings; that means also courses in, e.g., social science, political science, implementation science, health economics, etc. Broadening researchers' training will teach them not only how to do research but also what to research. Although most PhD research requires specialisation, there is only room for a small number of specialised researchers after their PhD and they are often required to develop a more generalist approach. Medical education should include acquaintance in a research or practical context with inequalities. Career pathways must encourage (and not punish) integration of disciplines. To make this attractive, the incentive system of research has to change. The current academic promotion system rewards individuals and focused research rather than teams and multidisciplinarity. Publishing in lower impact journals should not hamper academic career opportunities.

Fourth Solution: Funding for Research That Integrates the Three Approaches

This is only possible through influencing the research agendas of big funders at global and national levels. Cross-cutting research often ends up on the 'out of remit' list of funders focusing on just one area. It is a positive development that health systems are for the first time on the research agenda of the European Union research funding programme Horizon Europe. However, in many research funding organisations proposals from our three research areas tend to be judged in direct competition with biomedical research. Research proposals often have to promise *the* big breakthrough in understanding or treating a particular disease. Integrated research into health systems, health services, and population health will never lead to these kinds of big breakthroughs. Instead, it leads to conceptual changes and better understanding of interdependencies in health systems. With the direct competition with other fields of research, review panels are also often heterogeneous and have a lack of knowledge about health systems, health services, and population health research—let alone about the importance of their integration—and as a consequence judgements tend to be based on methodology and not on substance. This methodological orientation is a problem when their gold standard is the randomised controlled trial. Research proposals that propose to integrate our three areas of research may require reviewers that are acquainted with the three areas and thus more different reviewers (see Box 8.1).

> **Box 8.1 Funding in the Broad Area of Public Health Research**
> In January 2014, the main German research funding organisation, Deutsche Forschungsgemeinschaft, organised a round table on applying for, reviewing, and funding public health research. Here, public health research was understood to include health systems research, health services research, and population health research and epidemiology. A number of recommendations were made for researchers who apply for funding, review panellists, and the funding organisation. The results of this round table were later published. The summary of the points to be taken into account by review boards and funding organisations in public health research include the following:
>
> - Reviews on the often inter–/transdisciplinary proposals will usually be done by specialists in one discipline/method; if several disciplines and methods have been covered by different reviewers, encourage and moderate exchange among them.
> - Take into account the balance between internal and external validity of the research and acknowledge that research often takes place in complex real-life situations.
> - Be aware of the cumulative effect of critical remarks in reviews; the number of critical remarks is likely to increase with the number of theories and methods employed and the number of reviewers involved even if the quality of the project remains the same.
>
> Source: [7]

8.5 Conclusions

- The questions we pose and the issues we study in health systems, health services, and population health research are based on the problems that policymakers and practitioners encounter in health care sector of society.
- Our three fields are not the only areas in which research is siloed: health policy making at national and intermediate levels is also often fragmented, with, e.g., separate departments in ministries of health. This affects the 'demand' for integrated studies.
- Given the influence of health systems and health service provision on inequalities in population health, the reduction of these inequalities requires more than population-level interventions on the social determinants of health, although these are of unabated importance.
- Despite vested interests in the health system and in health service provision, health systems may be easier to change than societal structures of inequalities. However, the population health inequality impacts of health system changes are seldom analysed.

- Our whole-system approach of combining health systems, health services, and population health research has implications for research designs and methodology. We have formulated a number of elements for a research agenda.
- To improve collaboration between researchers in the three fields of research and to break down silos, we have discussed four areas where changes may contribute: the organisation of research, publication venues and conferences, capacity building and career opportunities, and finally the funding of research.

References

1. Leyland AH, Groenewegen PP. Multilevel analysis for public health and health services research: health in context. New York etc: Springer International Publishing; 2020.
2. Maassen H. Interview met Jan Kremer Medisch Contact 2024(8 augustus):20–3.
3. NASEM. Ending unequal treatment: strategies to achieve equitable health care and optimal health for all. Washington, DC: The National Academies Press; 2024.
4. Thomson LJM, Waterson H, Chatterjee HJ. Successes and challenges of partnership working to tackle health inequalities using collaborative approaches to communitybased research: mixed methods analysis of focus group evidence. Int J Equity Health. 2024;23:135.
5. Buxton M, Hanney S. How can payback from health services research be assessed? J Health Serv Res Policy. 1996;1(1):35–43.
6. Ari MD, Iskander J, Araujo J, Casey C, Kools J, Chen B, et al. A science impact framework to measure impact beyond journal metrics. PLoS One. 2020;15(12):e0244407.
7. Gerhardus A, Becher H, Groenewegen PP, Mansmann U, Meyer T, Pfaff H, et al. Applying for, reviewing and funding public health research in Germany and beyond. Health Res Policy Syst. 2016;14:43.

Open Access This chapter is licensed under the terms of the Creative Commons Attribution 4.0 International License (http://creativecommons.org/licenses/by/4.0/), which permits use, sharing, adaptation, distribution and reproduction in any medium or format, as long as you give appropriate credit to the original author(s) and the source, provide a link to the Creative Commons license and indicate if changes were made.

The images or other third party material in this chapter are included in the chapter's Creative Commons license, unless indicated otherwise in a credit line to the material. If material is not included in the chapter's Creative Commons license and your intended use is not permitted by statutory regulation or exceeds the permitted use, you will need to obtain permission directly from the copyright holder.

Index

A
Access, 2, 18, 24, 40, 51, 64, 79, 89
Accessibility, 15, 23, 34, 51, 53–56, 59, 60, 64, 66, 67, 69, 90, 93, 96
Agent-based models, 81, 84, 91
Artificial intelligence (AI), 71, 72

B
Benefits package, 30, 34, 35, 41, 57

C
Capacity building, 97, 99, 101
Care seeking, 82
Commercial determinants, 45

D
Decommodification, 28, 29
Dental care, 20, 41, 59, 96

E
Equality in health, 24, 30, 31, 41, 46, 55, 60, 75

F
Feedback, 18–21, 55, 79, 81, 83–84, 86, 96
Financing, 4, 5, 8, 17, 29, 30, 35, 41

H
Health expenditures, 29, 31, 42–43, 47, 60

Health impact analysis, 56, 81, 85, 86, 91, 92
Health inequalities, 1–4, 6–9, 15, 17, 18, 20, 21, 23, 25, 26, 28, 30, 41, 45, 51, 70, 71, 74, 79–86, 89, 90, 92–96, 100
Health inequalities accrual, 73–76
Health literacy, 18, 44, 53, 63, 64, 67–69, 73, 74
Health policy, 2–5, 24, 30, 35, 40, 56, 74, 83, 85, 91, 92, 97, 100
Health service provision, 3, 4, 8, 13, 15, 17, 18, 20, 51–60, 63–76, 92–95, 98, 100
Health services, 1, 13, 23, 39, 51, 63, 79, 89
Health services research, 1–9, 41, 82, 92, 94, 97, 98, 100
Health service utilisation, 8, 15, 20, 57, 79–86, 92, 95, 96
Health system coverage, 18–20, 25, 27–33, 41–43, 51, 57–60, 65, 90, 93, 96
Health system design, 3, 4, 8, 14, 15, 20, 23–35, 39–47, 51–60, 66, 92, 95, 96
Health systems, 1, 13, 23, 39, 51, 64, 79, 89
Health systems research, 1–9, 23, 39, 41, 95, 96, 100
Hospital care, 31, 34, 35

I
Inequity by disease, 72, 73
Intersectionality/intersectional, 7, 46, 81, 95, 98

L

Left-wing parties/government participation, 30, 32, 33, 35, 55, 90, 95
Levels of analysis, 13–17
Life course analysis, 17, 73–76, 79, 81, 86, 90, 96
Longitudinal analysis, 81, 83–84

M

Mental health care, 34, 59, 75, 96
Microsimulation, 81, 84–86, 91, 92
Multidisciplinary collaboration, 3, 8, 9, 97, 98

N

National health service (NH), 19, 25, 26, 28–30, 54, 57, 59, 96
Natural experiments, 19, 44, 81–83
Navigator, 44, 53

O

Out-of-pocket payment/costs, 27, 29, 42, 57–59, 89, 93

P

Pandemic, 15, 16, 33, 34, 54, 67, 85
Parallel systems, 20, 26, 27
Patient-provider relationship, 68
Policy, 3, 18, 24, 41, 55, 74, 83, 91
Political influence, 32, 55
Population health, 1, 13, 28, 39, 60, 79, 89
Population health research, 1–9, 91–95, 97–101
Populist radical right-wing (PRR), 33

Prevention, 3, 4, 8, 28, 30, 31, 34, 41, 43, 54, 60, 75, 76, 85, 93
Primary care, 20, 27, 43, 53, 67, 81, 89
Private health care/system, 25, 28, 30, 35, 60, 90
Public health foresight, 81, 85, 91, 92

Q

Quality of care, 53, 56, 59, 70, 71, 76

R

Research agenda, 20, 94–97, 99, 101
Research environments, 56, 70, 98
Research funding, 99, 100
Responsiveness, 15, 30, 41, 55, 84, 90

S

Social determinants of health, 2, 4, 13, 15, 17, 19, 23, 28, 31, 39, 41, 63, 70, 71, 83, 92–94, 100
Social health insurance (SHI), 25, 26, 28–31, 35, 53, 59, 89
Societal values, 6, 15, 17, 19, 20, 23–35, 39, 69
Systems science, 79, 86, 91

U

Universal health coverage (UHC), 18, 31–33, 42, 58, 60, 90, 93

W

Welfare systems, 19, 23, 28–29, 34, 89, 94

Made in the USA
Monee, IL
03 May 2026